D1460018

THE MINDFUL GEEK

Michael W. Taft

CEPHALOPOD
REX

2015

Cephalopod Rex Publishing
89 Kensington Rd.
Kensington, CA, 94707 USA

www.mindfulgeek.net
www.meditationwithmichael.com
www.deconstructingyourself.com

International Standard Book Number: 978-0692475386

Version number 001.00

"Until you make the unconscious conscious,
it will direct your life and you will call it fate."
~ C. G. Jung

CONTENTS

Acknowledgments

I'd like to thank my meditation teachers, Dhyanyogi Sri Madhusudandasji, Sri Anandi Ma Pathak, Dileepji Pathak, and Shinzen Young for all their love, patience, and guidance over the decades. Shinzen in particular has been instrumental in the ideas, formulations, and system presented in this book.

The Hindus have a saying that your first spiritual teacher is your mother, and that is certainly true in my case. Thanks, Mom. And thanks to my whole family.

Thanks to Thomas Metzinger, Judson Brewer, Dave Vago, and Richie Davidson for serving as friends and inspiration, and for their research and thought leadership which is moving the field forward.

Thanks to Sandra Aamodt, Bridgette Anderson, Al Billings, Gareth Branwyn, Bill Duane, Braxton Dudley, Jessica Graham, Sean Dae Houlihan, Todd Mertz, Julianna Raye, Zachary Schlosser, Corey Swartsel, Lindsay Stärke, Ishan Walpola, and Erik Yates all contributed vital notes, feedback, and enthusiasm that helped to greatly improve this text. And thanks to Troy Coll, Carol Schneck Varner, and Emily Yates for proofreading above and beyond the call of duty.

Thank you to Bill Duane and Michael Van Riper for giving me the opportunity to field-test so many of these ideas and teaching methods with the übergeeks at Google.

Thanks to Rick Hanson for his unflagging and deeply enthusiastic support. Peter Baumann for making so many things possible, and for keeping things interesting. Corey Swartsel, Douglas McLeod, Ellen Balis, Maurizio and Zaya Benazzo, Amy Hertz, Amber Rickert, Jessica Graham, and Rick Jarow for being wonderful human beings.

Thank you to Morgan Blackledge and Laura V. Ward, who have been friends on this journey of awakening ever since the old days in East Lansing. *Requiescat in pace*, Robert Nash.

Thank you to Krisztina Lazar and Ernst Schmidt for helping to conceive and design the exterior. Thanks to Gareth Branwyn for editing the final manuscript, and for contributing so much experience and help to the crowdfunding campaign. Hail, Eris!

A deep thanks to all my students over the years who have taught me so much, and for being such fierce, brave, and loving people.

Very special thanks to Krisztina Lazar.

Finally, the creation of *The Mindful Geek* was made possible by the generous contributions of many individuals to its Indiegogo funding campaign. I'd like to thank the following people, as well as many others who wished to remain anonymous. My apologies if I have inadvertently left anybody off of this list.

Adam Farasati, Adam Pfenninberger, Allison Ayer, Alvin Alexander, Ana Rubio, Andrea Lazar, Arrowyn Husom, Audrey M Korman, Bianca Petrie, Bobby L Bessey, Boris Schepker, Brent Cullimore, Brian Baker, Brian P Rumburg, Bridgette Anderson, Brooks M Dunn, Charlotte Kay, Christine Rener, Cory Smith, Cyril Gojer, Damian Frank, Daniel Abramovich, Daniel B Horton, Daniel L Ruderman, Daragh J Byrne, Darin Olien, David B Tierkel, Denise G Ellard, Dianne Powers Wright, Dominick Pesola, Donniel Thomas, Douglas McLeod, Elan J Frenkel, Elvira Gonzalez, Emily Barrett, Emily Yates, Eric Klein, Erin Diehm, F F Seeburger, Francesca de Wolfe de Wytt, Francis Lacoste Julien, Gareth Branwyn, George R Haas, Gil Evans, Giuseppe Falconio, Glenda K. Lippmann, Heidi E Clippard, Heidi Hardner, Hirofumi Hashimoto, Hulkko Heikki, Isabelle C Lecomte, Jacqueline Nichols, Jamie L Rowe, Jeanette Cournoyer, Jessica Clark-Graham, Joan T Sherwood, Joel Bentley, John B Rasor, Jonathan Schmitt, Joy C Daniels, Judy N Munsen, K A Berry, Karen Cowe, Karen Yankosky, Kaycee Flinn, Kenneth Britten,

Kenneth Lalonde, Kestrel C Lancaster, Laura Saaf, Laura V Ward, Lauren Monroe, Laurie Morrow, Linda L. Small, Linda Read, Lindsay M Stärke, Lisa J Brayton, Loren W Smith II, Louis Billings, Lydia Leovic Towery, Mark J. Miller, Mark K. Glorie, Marsha E Parkhill, Micah Daigle, Michael Baranowski, Michele P Berry, Michelle L Lyon, Yogi Nataraja Kallio, Nick R Woods, Noah J Hittner, Pamala Lewis, Paula A Zittere, Peter H Goh, Pokkrong Promsurin, Qadir Timerghazin, Randy Johnson, Rebecca L. Johnson, Richard Miller, Robert D Larson, Robert Y Smith Jr, Saiesh C Reddy, Samuel D Brown, Sanjeev Singh Guram, Sara A. Sporer, Scott R Petersen, Sharad Jaiswal, Shyamaa Creaven, Stefan Kahlert, Stephen Wharmby, Stina Stiernstrom, Sue Kretschmann, Susan Whitman, Suzanne Rice, Timothy Boudreau, Todd Sattersten, Troy Coll, Tyler Osborn, Volkmar Kirchner, William D Culman, William Duane, William H Taft Jr, Willow Pearson, and Zachary Schlosser

Introduction

From Zen temples in Japan to yogi caves in India, I've been meditating for over thirty years. As a result, I have extensive experience in both Buddhist and Hindu meditation traditions. I started in the late 70s, because I was experiencing so much teenage anxiety. Meditation gave me some relief, and I was hooked. In the 1990s, I worked as editorial director for Sounds True, a publishing company specializing in spiritual and psychological teaching programs. While there, I had the good fortune to meet dozens of the most popular and interesting spiritual teachers in the world. I produced their programs, which meant that I got exposed to the workings of dozens of traditions.

At Sounds True, I met an American meditation teacher named Shinzen Young[1] and helped to create his classic program *The Science of Enlightenment*. I found his style of teaching, which was both science-oriented and ecumenical, attractive for a number of reasons which deeply resonated with me. While nominally a Buddhist, he could talk intelligently about the spiritual practices of many religions and traditions. He was also a geek—fascinated by dead languages and abstract mathematics. I liked his modern, rational, and non-sectarian viewpoint.

I have studied and worked with Shinzen for several decades now, and I am currently a senior facilitator in the Basic Mindfulness system he created. Basic Mindfulness is by far the most comprehensive and industrial-strength meditation system I've encountered. Much of what you'll find in this book is Basic Mindfulness,[2] and you have Shinzen to thank for the real clarity and brilliance behind these techniques. I have altered the system in several respects, however, in order to make it more accessible and friendly to those whom we might call "mindful geeks," and also to fit my own teaching style, methods, and predilections.

About ten years ago, a friend asked me if I would consider teaching him, and a group of people he knew, how to meditate. Having had to work through so many of my own difficulties the hard way, I was happy to give others the best of tools and the skills I had learned to help improve their lives. Our society doesn't prepare people to deal with most of the challenges we actually end up facing. Stress, overwhelm, constant worry, the breakup of meaningful relationships, death of loved ones—these are just a few of the aspects of life that our schooling never addresses. I can only imagine how much a meditation class in high school, even as an after school activity, would have helped me with my significant childhood anxiety. We receive no formal training in emotional regulation, ability to focus, healthy forms of relaxation, nor in a dozen or so skills that would be invaluable to ourselves and society. Having gone out and acquired these skills on my own, I could see how others around me could benefit from them too.

I wanted to share so much of what I'd learned, but the world had changed since I began this journey. I had learned meditation within the traditions—chanting in temples, meditating in caves, taking pilgrimages high in the Himalayas, worshipping deities. But the people who asked me to teach them meditation were usually uninterested in the "spiritual" aspects. They were mainly younger, tech-oriented individuals, many of whom had come out of the punk/alternative/art scene, who were not about to get into the esoteric practices I'm so fond of, or enter the worldview of another culture quite that deeply. They wanted to gain the benefits of the practice without drinking the Kool Aid.

As chance would have it, my own thoughts and practice were evolving along similar lines. While I loved (and still do) the spiritual, religious, and cultural practices around meditation, I found myself increasingly drawn to exploring the more psychological and neurological understandings of it, and the human brain in general. Starting around 2000, I became very interested in what neuroscience and evidence-based psychology had to say about meditative states and practices. I had the good fortune to work with Peter Baumann to develop the Being Human project,[3] which put me in touch with some of the leading researchers in the field, such as Richie Davidson, Judson Brewer, David Eagleman, among many others; psychologists Paul Ekman and Helen Fisher, as well as philosophers such as Thomas Metzinger.

Under the influence of such luminaries, I gradually completely reworked my understanding of the wild and woolly experiences of meditation I'd enjoyed in the traditional schools into a structured, secular, science-based model. That made it possible to share my knowledge with the Silicon Valley tech wizards I was meeting in the Bay Area and elsewhere. I now teach meditation at Google and some of the other largest corporations in the world. The arc of my own development, together with working at such places, as well as the influence of Shinzen, has led to the material in this book.

If you are a religious practitioner of meditation, belonging to a Buddhist, Hindu, or other tradition, I want to make it clear that I'm not attacking nor discarding those teachings. I have dedicated the majority of my life to learning and practicing those ways, and I deeply honor them. The point of this book is to offer the practice of meditation to people who are turned off by that sort of thing, and so would otherwise never take up meditation. In the spirit of making the world a better place and helping to relieve suffering wherever we find it, I think that meditation must be taught to anyone who's interested. If that sometimes means separating it from its religious and cultural contexts, so be it. The temples will still be standing, giving their colorful and fragrant offerings to those who wish to partake.

In the meantime, for all the "thinkers, doers, and makers," out there, the mindful geeks, here is a book about meditation I wrote just for you.

Michael
Berkeley, Summer 2015

CHAPTER ONE

The Power of Meditation

You've seen the hype. From the cover of the *New York Times* magazine to a *60 Minutes* episode starring Anderson Cooper, mindfulness meditation is touted as the latest panacea to humanity's ills. Hardly a day goes by when there isn't some new hyperbolic article claiming that another scientific study proves that mindfulness meditation cures cancer, collapses quantum wave functions, or will thrust you into the ranks of the ultra-rich in just one year.

With such rabid hoopla focused on a buzzword—mindfulness!—you'd be excused for wondering if there was anything substantial behind all this aggressive publicity about a simple meditation technique. Can mindfulness meditation really deliver or is all this just some New Age marketing scam? Is there any *there* there?

In short, the answer is a resounding Yes, mindfulness meditation can deliver on many of the reasonable benefits you've heard about. As far as I know, it doesn't cure cancer, make you rich, or collapse quantum states. But assuming that you put in the time and energy that the practice requires, it's likely that you'll get some of the advertised benefits, such as increased concentration, creativity, and productivity, reduced stress, improved mood, better relationships, and increased health and wellbeing.

How do I know? First, from my own experience. I started meditating over 30 years ago. As a teenager in Michigan, I suffered crippling anxiety attacks, and couldn't find any help for my situation. Eventually, I started meditating, and that brought some relief right away. I had fewer anxiety attacks, and I could cope much better with the ones that I did have. They were shorter and less intense.

After that, I was hooked, and in the decades since then I have found that meditation has drastically improved my life. It's still life, with all its ups and downs, but I'm much better at enjoying the ups and navigating the downs than I ever could have imagined.

Secondly, there's the experience of people I know. For the past decade, I've been teaching meditation to hundreds of people in homes, in classes, at various retreat centers, and at companies like Google. Over the years with these students, I've witnessed similar results: if they put in the time, they experience many of the benefits of mindfulness meditation for themselves.

Thirdly, for thousands of years, people from different cultures on different continents with limited communication between each other all claimed that meditation practices changed their lives for the better. You don't have to believe them, but it would be irresponsible to reject such claims out of hand—especially given that such similar ideas come from very different sources. Anecdotes aren't evidence, but it's something to keep in mind.

Finally, current brain science and psychology backs up many of these claims about meditation with some fairly robust findings. In the last decade in particular, the number of serious research studies involving mindfulness has skyrocketed. Part of the reason for this scientific interest is that so much of the research hits paydirt. That is, mindfulness meditation does what it says on the box often enough that scientists have become intrigued, and the funding for such research has increased dramatically.

So what can mindfulness meditation actually do for you? Even a cursory summary of such research would take up a whole book, but here is just the briefest glance at a few of the benefits that are provably real. With guidance and a committed practice, over time, mindfulness meditation has been shown to:

Improve Your Focus — Focus is a trainable skill, and meditation systematically trains you to concentrate. This increase in concentration ability doesn't just happen when you're meditating, but continues all day long as you go about your business. Mindfulness's positive effect on focus has been demonstrated in this long-term study,[4] and this study,[5] and has even been shown to make a big difference in novice meditators after only ten days.[6]

Concentration is, in fact, one of the core skills of meditation, and there are dozens or hundreds more studies that support its role in improving concentration. An important early study[7] by neuroscientist Richard Davidson at the University of Wisconsin shows that meditation makes attentional resources much more flexible, which means you can concentrate more powerfully.

Reduce Your Stress — We've all heard that meditation can help you to relax and become less stressed out. It's a proven way to trigger the body's parasympathetic response,[8] which eases you into a less tense state. When your hands are too shaky to guide yet another cup of coffee to your lips without spilling it, meditation is just what you need.

Many of these studies are done in laboratory environments, but one fascinating study with human resources personnel in a high-stress, real-world environment showed that mindfulness meditation could even make very stressful situations easier to handle.[9] It lowers your cortisol levels[10]—the main hormone implicated in the body's stress response. A 2010 meta-analysis of 39 studies found that mindfulness is a useful intervention for treating anxiety[11] and mood disorders. An even more recent study[12] (2014) showed that mindfulness was just as powerful as cognitive-behavioral therapy in treating anxiety and depression.

Enhance Your Empathy — Mindfulness meditation will help you connect to other people. One practice is called compassion meditation, in which you focus on feelings of love and empathy. Experiments show that over time this can dramatically boost your empathy[13] (sense of emotional connection) with others. Medical students under intense stress report higher levels of empathy[14] when they meditate.

Freedom from Automatic Reactions — How long does it take you to recover from an upsetting event? Mindfulness can reduce that time measurably,[15] and get you back on track faster after emotional upheavals.[16] Recovery from emotional upsets is a key feature of resilience, the ability to bounce back in the face of adversity. It also makes you able to be less of a dick to people in general, because you won't react so fast or so mechanically to the usual triggers, but will instead have some ability to think before you react.

Increase Your Cognitive Flexibility — Mindfulness meditation has been shown to increase "cognitive flexibility,"[17] which means it allows you to see the world in a new way and behave differently than you have in the past. It helps you to respond to negative or stressful situations more skillfully. This boosts creativity and innovation, allowing you to have more "aha!" experiences,[18] as well as original thinking.[19] Using the attention strategy known as "open monitoring" particularly enhances creativity and originality. We'll look at open monitoring in the chapter called "The Brain's Screensaver."

Boost Your Memory — The number of facts you can hold in your head at once—what scientists call "working memory"—is a crucial aspect of effectiveness in learning, problem solving, and organization. A study of military personnel under stress showed that those who practiced meditation experienced an increase in working memory[20] as well as feeling better than those who didn't meditate. Another study showed that it not only improves memory, but boosts test scores, too.[21] Even practicing mindfulness for as little as four days may improve memory and other cognitive skills.[22]

Make You Less Sensitive to Pain — Mindfulness meditation changes your physical brain structure in many ways; one is that it may actually increase the thickness of your cortex,[23] and reduce your sensitivity to pain.[24]

Give You a Better Brain — Mindfulness trains the prefrontal lobe area of your brain (it may actually get bigger),[25] as well as enhancing other areas which give the benefits of an entire package of related functions[26] such as self-insight, morality, intuition, and fear modulation. While research doesn't prove definite causation, practicing meditation predicts above-average cortical thickness, and how long subjects have been practicing meditation is directly correlated with how much above average their cortex thickness is. The pain study listed above also demonstrates that mindfulness practice does increase gray matter density in the brain. It's also shown to "slow, stall, or even reverse age-related neurodegeneration,"[27] meaning that it's a guard against some of the most humiliating ravages of old age.[28]

The long list above represents just a few of the positive ways mindfulness meditation has been demonstrated to improve quality of life. There are even deeper and more powerful benefits that we will examine later. But just looking at this list, it's clear that mindfulness meditation can really make a difference in how you feel each day, how effective you are in reaching your goals, how well you get along with other people, and more.

Not bad for a practice that involves simply paying attention to your own sensory experience. Although many of the studies listed involve people doing intensive practice many hours a day, there is compelling evidence that even practicing half an hour a day can make a big difference.

If you are a card-carrying geek, however, the upside of all these possible benefits may be strongly counterbalanced by the downside of having to deal with religion, spirituality, or other things you may consider nonsense. Mindfulness meditation is mainly associated with Buddhist religion, and for that reason can seem deeply suspect to skeptical, rational people.

I'm here to lay that worry to rest. In my experience, you can get many of the benefits of meditation without joining any religion, going to church, or believing in reincarnation or karma. By treating mindfulness as a scientifically-based, psychological technique, you can keep your atheistic or agnostic secular skepticism and still maintain a powerful, regular, and deeply effective meditation practice.

Meditation is really a technology. And like any good technology, if you use it correctly, it will do the job reliably whether you believe in it or not. At its heart, meditation is a technology for hacking the human wetware in order to improve your life. And this book is a manual for how to make the most of that technology for yourself. Let's look more deeply now at what meditation actually is.

CHAPTER TWO

Meditation and Mindfulness

It may sound a little strange or precious to call meditation a "technology," but that's an accurate term. The *Merriam-Webster Dictionary* defines a technology as "the practical application of knowledge, especially in a particular area." Meditation, as a practical application of psychology to the area of human wellbeing and performance, fits the definition. Also, I'm calling meditation a technology because it gets you thinking about the true nature of the practice.

Meditation is one of those words that means a lot of different things. That's not really so unusual for a technology, however. Think of the term "telephone" and you'll see what I mean. A telephone can mean anything from a hand-cranked device with a megaphone, to a Bluetooth rig, to the most current smartphone.

And yet we all understand why these very different devices are called a "telephone." It's because one person can talk and listen to another through them. If you're doing that, then it's a telephone. If you're also seeing the person, however, that's something different.

In the same way, meditation can mean a wide range of different practices. Some of these practices seem to be the opposite of each other, or mutually exclusive. For example, there is the technique known as mantra meditation. In mantra meditation, the practitioner mentally repeats a certain syllable, word, or sentence over and over. He or she fills up the mind with specific verbal thoughts. But in other forms of meditation, the idea is to have *no* verbal thoughts in the mind at all. How can *both* of these techniques be meditation? It would seem to be a complete contradiction, yet they're both meditation, and are both effective to various degrees.

So what are the essential aspects that make meditation meditation? In my opinion, the essence of meditation is that it is *a psychological practice which makes the unconscious conscious and which improves life.*

What does it mean to improve life? For the purposes of this book, let's call it something that makes you happier, healthier, and more effective. Those are some nice, concrete categories. We'll leave aside any conjectures about "spiritual" improvement or growth as outside the scope of this book. Instead we'll only look at things that benefit you in one or all of these practical ways. Is it making you happier, healthier, and more effective or not? Is it reducing stress, helping you sleep soundly, and improving your relationships, or not?

For anyone involved in meditation, I recommend applying these criteria every single day to your practice. If it's not improving your life, in a way that you can experience relatively quickly, then I recommend switching practices to something that does. Imaginary benefit is no benefit at all.

What does it mean to make the unconscious conscious? It means that meditation calls your attention to things you wouldn't have noticed otherwise. It gives you insights, in other words. The conscious part of your brain only constitutes a minority percentage of brain activity.

The majority of your brain function is going on "under the hood" of conscious awareness.

Scientists used to believe that your neurons remained at rest until called upon for a task. So if you were just hanging out on a porch, looking at some scenery, say, a large portion of your brain would be inactive at that moment. Recent studies paint a very different picture. When you switch from just gazing at the scenery to some highly focused task like reading, there is, at most, only a small percentage change in additional energy required. In other words, the brain is "on" all the time, and most of the energy consumed by the brain is for activities you are unaware of—even when you are daydreaming or sleeping.

This "always-on" activity of the brain is known as the "default mode"—meaning that it's what the brain is doing when you're not busy with anything else. Note that this is totally different from the old—and much debunked—claim that you "only use ten percent of your brain." Here I'm saying that only some portion of brain activity is available to consciousness. The rest is occurring behind the scenes, so to speak.

And when you think about it, that's a good thing. A large amount of your brain is dedicated to keeping your body running properly, for example. Would you really want to make the effort to consciously monitor and adjust blood sugar levels, heart rate, flush response, and the details of stomach digestion all the time? It's pretty convenient that your brain handles all that tedious bookkeeping out of sight.

A few of those things can be brought into conscious awareness with some practice, but those are not really what I'm talking about. Becoming intimately aware of the process of stomach digestion, for example, would probably detract from quality of life rather than add to it. It would be extremely tedious, and you might screw it up. Evolution has provided our organisms with excellent systems that take care of such background processes automatically, thank you.

But there are other processes, other systems, other decisions, going on behind the scenes that it would really benefit you to be aware of. One powerful example is your emotional responses. Emotions control your entire life. You spend all your efforts trying to change bad emotions into good ones, or to make the good ones stronger and longer lasting. A human being can be modeled as a machine that seeks to make itself feel better emotionally.

The trouble is, very few of us can tell with any accuracy what we're feeling in any given moment. And yet, these emotions are completely regulating your behavior in the background. You are being steered by something that is largely outside of your conscious awareness—and that means that you don't consciously know what's actually going on with your own guidance system, and cannot predict your behavior.

This is an obvious problem, and is one of the unconscious things that meditation can help by bringing it into conscious awareness. When you use meditation to become more aware of what you're feeling, the unconscious or semi-conscious flavors of emotional experience begin to come into focus. Your own motivations and drives become clearer. Not just in a conceptual way, but in a way you can physically detect, moment by moment, throughout your day. This is the essence of emotional intelligence, and it is life changing.

Mindfulness meditation probably achieves this self-knowledge by actually *growing the relevant areas of your brain*. In the case of contacting your own feelings, the crucial area of the brain is known as the *insula*.[29] You have one insula in each hemisphere of your brain, and the job of these structures is to allow you to detect your own internal body sensations (a skill known as *interoception*), as well as processing social emotions and even orgasms. A large number of studies have demonstrated that when you meditate, your insula grows larger and more convoluted.[30] In other words, your brain actually gets better at consciously feeling what you're feeling. You've got more processing power to bring to bear, more cycles per second to apply to the job.

The first time you have even a small, fleeting experience of direct contact with your own previously unconscious emotional responses—something which an average person can achieve in just a few days of meditating for 30 minutes per day—you will be surprised that you ever lived without it. It's like there has been a secret control room running behind the curtain your whole life, and you have just pulled aside the curtain. You get to feast your eyes on the wonder of your own internal guidance system.

Eventually, with enough practice, you will not have to make do with occasional glimpses into this control room, but will be able to monitor it as often and in as much detail as you like. Even this beginning level of insight into an unconscious process can improve the experience of your own life. (We'll talk more about exactly how this works in the chapter on emotions.)

Gaining insight into your unconscious emotional responses is just one example. There are many other possibilities, such as learning to consciously relax, learning to consciously appreciate external sensory perception, learning to consciously experience pleasure, and more.

And meditation doesn't just give you insight into yourself; it gives you insight into other people as well. As research shows, the insula doesn't just help you feel your own feelings. It is also instrumental in helping you detect what other people are feeling.[31] This can result in much better relationships, as well as an enhanced ability to read other people—and who couldn't use that?

Gaining insights into yourself and those around you is a really useful skill. In the early 1990s, I built personal computers for a small tech start up in Boulder, Colorado. Our bread and butter was putting together XTs, but every once in a while, I'd construct a "screaming-fast" 486 with a monstrous 40MB (*not* GB) hard drive. All the guys in the shop would gather around this miraculous device and we'd watch it piece together a color Mandelbrot fractal, one achingly slow pixel at a time. After that, I got into Linux and even coded a few humble applications in Java, Python, and Objective-C.

Over the years, I've found that the little bit of knowledge I have about what goes on under the hood of a computer has actually saved me a lot of time, money, and headaches, as well as being kind of fun.

I feel something similar about meditation practice. Meditation teaches you to examine your everyday sensory experience very closely. The insights into your own motivations, drives, and behavior you get from doing that regularly is quite illuminating and helpful in your life. I call this feature of meditation the "under the hood" benefit.

So, when we talk about meditation of any kind, it makes conscious something that was previously unconscious, and it does so to the betterment of your life. In this sense, it can be seen as an awareness-extending technology, something like a microscope or a telescope. It allows you to see (or hear or feel) aspects of sensory experience which were previously unavailable to you. And it does this not through some kind of magic, but through the wonder of neuroplasticity.

Neuroplasticity and Attention

For a very long time, scientists thought that the human brain was born as a *tabula rasa* ("blank slate") upon which learning could write anything at all. Children could be taught any subject, but once a person reached adulthood, their brain was set in stone. No big changes were possible after that, and no new neurons could grow. You were stuck with what you had.

This was the state of neuroscience up until the 1970s, when some compelling experiments convinced scientists to rethink this aspect of the brain. One classic experiment by Paul Bach-y-Rita involved congenitally blind people who had never seen anything in their lives. Bach-y-Rita installed rows of vibrating pins in the backrest of a special dentist's chair. This grid of 400 pins was connected to a huge video camera mounted on a wheeled base. A bank of computers took the electrical signal from the video camera and used it to fire the grid of vibrating pins. When subjects sat in the chair, they could feel this grid of pins on their backs, and sense whether each pin was moving or still. Pictures of this contraption are truly terrifying, especially with the rather Frankensteinian-looking 1960s technology of the jury-rigged dentist's chair.[32]

Despite its horror-movie good looks (which the participants couldn't see anyway), the chair did something remarkable: it allowed blind people to "see" images with the skin of their backs. They eventually got so good at it that they could distinguish a picture of 1960s fashion icon Twiggy from other images. The brain was able to take touch sensations from the skin and learn to interpret them in the visual cortex, turning it into visual information. Touch sensations from the skin are not normally processed in the visual cortex, of course, but in these people, the brain had retrained itself to do so.[33]

This clever experiment demonstrated that the adult brain was capable of amazing changes. This result shook the scientific world, and soon, more research was pouring in that showed that our brains continue to alter, update, and rewire themselves throughout our adult lives. Neuroplasticity is behind the famous phrase "neurons that fire together, wire together," which describes the mechanism by which neuroplasticity occurs. When neurons fire together, they form a new network, which then enhances the brain's ability to perform that activity in the future.

And the brain does this much more than anybody imagined at first. Even something as simple as learning a new word, we now understand, involves an actual change in the neuronal structure of the brain. All learning is neuroplasticity at work. For example, one study taught participants to use Morse code, which caused increased activity and gray matter density in the portion of the brain associated with reading.[34]

The ramifications of that statement ("All learning is neuroplasticity") are immense. It means that you can almost "sculpt" your brain in an intentional and directed manner. Whatever you focus your attention on, regularly over time, will change the brain itself—physically alter it, some parts becoming larger or smaller—to get better at processing the thing you're focusing on. Within limitations, you can make the brain you want.

A famous example of such brain sculpting was revealed by an experiment conducted in the 1990s on London taxi drivers. London grew willy-nilly for thousands of years. Streets were added here and there, any which way, without any overarching plan. So there is no way to reduce the map of London's streets to some kind of heuristic. You just have to learn all of the streets by heart—an epic feat of memorization that takes several years. And to get licensed as a London cabby, you have to take an exam to *prove* that you've memorized them.

Memorization of spatial information uses a specific region of the brain, known as the hippocampus. Using brain scans, Dr. Eleanor Maguire of the University College London showed that the hippocampus in London cab drivers was markedly larger than those in control subjects. [35] Furthermore, the longer the cabby had been on the job, the bigger their hippocampus. Maguire noted "the hippocampus has changed its structure to accommodate their huge amount of navigating experience." [36]

In other words, merely by focusing their attention on their navigation skills, London cabbies were able to grow the relevant structure in their brain. They modified their brains to become better at their jobs.

You can sculpt your brain to become better at virtually anything, including having a better life. By using practices to direct your attention at specific things (like your breath, your emotions, or your sense of relaxation), you can leverage neuroplasticity to enhance the relevant aspects of your experience. You do this just like London cabbies do, by focusing on the right things, over and over, for a long period of time.

Not all of us are going to memorize the street map of London for a living, so how does this apply specifically to meditation? Researchers had participants, who had never meditated before, undergo an eight week course in mindfulness meditation. They experienced gray matter increases in brain regions associated with "learning and memory processes, emotion regulation, self-referential processing, and perspective-taking"—precisely the sorts of functions we might expect to get better at by practicing meditation.[37] Mindfulness meditation, then, trains you to get better at some of the very things that will increase your sense of wellbeing.

What Is Mindfulness?

That's where mindfulness comes in. You'll have noticed that I've been talking a lot about meditation, but the title of this book is *The Mindful Geek* and not *The Meditative Geek*. A few times I've used the phrase "mindfulness meditation," without having made any distinction about what makes it different from other types of meditation.

What is the difference between meditation and mindfulness? Why use two different words? In short, mindfulness is a type of meditation, a subset of meditation. Specifically, *mindfulness means paying attention to your present-moment sensory experience in a nonjudgmental manner.* That's the basic definition.

The way the word is used in modern America, mindfulness not only means to meditate, but can also mean a way of directing attention in everyday life, even when you're not practicing formal meditation.

"Mindfulness" is the modern American translation of at least two words from the ancient Pali[38] language: *vipassana* and *sati*. When we're talking about a type of meditation, mindfulness represents the term *vipassana*, which actually means "insight" or "clear seeing" in Pali. This technique (really a whole group of techniques) is sometimes called insight meditation or vipassana.

When we're talking about a way of directing attention at any time, during formal meditation or not, mindfulness is the translation of the Pali term *sati*. Sati actually means "mindfulness," to pay close attention to what you're doing. To go even deeper, sati literally means "to remember," as in "to remember to pay attention to what you're doing."

If I were being a bit pedantic, I might note that it's a slight misnomer to call a meditation technique "mindfulness meditation." Strictly, the technique is "insight meditation," (*vipassana*) which involves using a lot of mindfulness (*sati*). Nowadays, however, it's normal in American English to call what we're doing mindfulness meditation. I actually prefer it. To use it in this way emphasizes a departure from its religious roots. Furthermore, these sorts of techniques belonged to other, separate traditions as well, and so it's not the case that only the Buddhist terms are the correct ones.[39]

When I use the term mindfulness, it can mean a type of meditation or a way of being in the world. In the best-case scenario, you will end up doing both of these kinds of mindfulness: formal sitting practice and practice in life.

Now that we know what mindfulness means, we can upgrade our definition of meditation to specifically address mindfulness meditation. Our new, improved definition that we'll be using goes as follows: *mindfulness meditation is a psychological technique that involves paying attention to your present-moment sensory experience in a nonjudgmental manner, and which makes the unconscious conscious for the purpose of improving your life.*

The system of mindfulness meditation that you'll learn in this book will direct your attention toward the things that will allow you to get the benefits of the practice.

What Mindfulness Meditation Is Not

My experience teaching meditation to thousands of people over the last decade has taught me that there are several misconceptions about mindfulness meditation. These misconceptions can really get in the way, so I'm just going to dispel them as quickly as possible right at the start.

The first is that mindfulness meditation means to "clear your mind" or to "have no thoughts." Nothing could be further from the truth. In mindfulness meditation, it doesn't matter how much thinking is going on during the meditation. It literally doesn't figure into the equation. The goal is not to empty your mind of thoughts; the goal is to pay attention to some aspect of your current sensory experience.

That means that you could actually be having a lot of thoughts, and still be having a perfectly good mindfulness meditation. So please do not worry at all, or think that you are doing it wrong, if you are having thoughts during mindfulness meditation.

Remember that there are a lot of different kinds of meditation. And some of these techniques do, in fact, ask you to clear your mind. For some reason, those techniques became one of our cultural images of what meditation is about, and that's unfortunate, because "stopping thinking" is not only very difficult to do, even for an advanced meditator, it's also not all that useful. So just let go of that image completely.

The second misconception is that meditation is something that is supposed to be blissful or pleasurable. The cultural image attached to this idea is that of a yogi seated in full lotus posture, fingers curled into a mudra (gesture) of perfection, face suffused with radiant ecstasy. The process of meditation, in this misconception, involves disappearing into a cloud of bliss.

Again, nothing could be further from the case. Mindfulness meditation involves paying attention to your present moment sensory experience nonjudgmentally. That counts no matter if your present-moment sensory experience is painful or pleasant, positive or negative. Rather than acting like Ren wearing the "happy helmet" (from the Ren & Stimpy episode "Stimpy's Invention"), in mindfulness meditation, you welcome whatever experience is arising, whether it's "happy, happy, joy, joy," or not.

It's possible to have a perfectly good mindfulness meditation while meditating on the body sensations of a headache, for example, or sitting in line at the DMV. There is no need to invoke, produce, or expect any sort of bliss. If bliss happens, that's fine, but you're not trying for it, and you're not trying to hold onto it if it does arise. That's the nonjudgmental part.

There's no stipulation that meditation must be done sitting cross-legged on the floor, either. Meditating while sitting in a chair works fine, too. No incense, candles, bells, or shawls required.

Mindfulness meditation involves paying attention to your present-moment sensory experience in a nonjudgmental way. It doesn't mean stopping thinking, emptying your mind, or feeling blissful. Thoughts and negative feeling are fine, if they arise.

We now know what mindfulness meditation is and is not. In general, there are two ways to practice it. Formal meditation means sitting quietly and motionless, doing the practice internally. Many people close their eyes while they do this. Meditation in motion means bringing mindfulness techniques into parts or moments of your everyday life, while driving, walking, or waiting, for example.

In this book, you'll learn how to do both of these meditation forms. You'll learn a whole series of specific mindfulness meditation practices, which you'll be able to practice on your own any time you want. I will also teach you the background and theory of meditation, as well as share with you many hints and tips that I've gleaned over decades of working with this material. Most of what's "hard" about meditation involves learning how to overcome the pitfalls, blind-alleys, cul-de-sacs, and misunderstandings along this path. I'll do my best to make sure you avoid these.

The goal is to get you meditating 30 minutes a day, at least five days a week. That's an achievable goal for most people. At that level, you'll begin to get the advertised benefits of mindfulness meditation very quickly (a month or two at most), and be able to sustain and grow those benefits over time. Of course, it's not required that you do that much. Even 10 minutes a day will get you far.

CHAPTER THREE

First Practice

I'm passionate about riding my bicycle on the weekends. I strap on a helmet, turn on a tracking app, and take off pedaling in the Berkeley hills. The heavy breathing, the coursing sweat, the thrill of flying downhill—I love it. Sometimes I ride for hours, but in the end, I'm just another weekend cyclist.

Many of my friends in the area are, by contrast, cycling *freaks*. They ride their bicycles hundreds of miles a week. These guys and gals are serious competitors. Let's just say their hair is permanently shaped like a honeycomb. So when we get together for coffee or dinner, I'm careful never to mention cycling. One inadvertent use of the word "bike" is enough to trigger an impromptu cycling-nerd gear forum. Minutia of front fork tuning and service intervals are discussed. Vehement altercations concerning the additional weight of 58mm carbon rims versus their improved aerodynamics. Aspects of diet related to automated interval training apps. We're talking Transmissions from Planet Velodrome.

And while, yes, bicycle shop talk can sometimes eighty-six all other conversation, I actually appreciate it. These are not people who just like to flap their jaws about this stuff for no reason. They are not armchair cyclists who brush the cobwebs off their beach cruiser once a year to trundle off after an ice cream cone under their sunhats. These are cycling *monsters*. The bicycle is a technology they actually *use*, practically every day, and of all the gear nerdery is a necessary and useful aspect of that lifestyle. All those little details really matter because that's how you get the most out of cycling.

Meditation is like a bicycle in that sense: it's a technology you *use*. It's meant to get you somewhere—to a life of enhanced wellbeing—it's something that you *live*. All the talk, all of the nerding out on details of practice, mental states, neuroscience, and so on, is all secondary to the doing of it. The actual practice of sitting down and meditating.

The goal of this book is to help you garner the benefits of mindfulness meditation, and to do that you have to do the practice. In essence, this is a practical book, almost a manual or handbook of mindfulness meditation. Although you will find a lot of complex, detailed, esoteric-seeming information about meditation in here (Transmissions from Planet Meditation) it's only here because if you are meditating every day—really making mindfulness a functioning, growing, useful part of your life-improvement plan—then these are the kinds of minutia that become of functional interest to you.

And yet it's all for the sake of doing the practice. Imagine making somebody read a whole book on riding bicycles before he or she ever felt the wind in their hair, the speed-elation as they flew down a big hill, the satisfaction of grinding up a steep grade. The book would be almost meaningless, because they wouldn't have an experiential sense of what it was all about.

So, before we go any further, let's get down to the real business with an actual meditation practice. Let's get our hands dirty, our boots wet, with some real-life sitting meditation. Don't worry, O Geeky One, it won't hurt. And you'll have the satisfaction of having given it a go. More to the point, you'll have a much better idea of what the rest of this book is actually about. So fire up your neurons and get ready for a little meditation workout.

In later chapters, we'll get into posture, we'll get into theory, we'll get into variations and special exercises. But let's just leave all that alone for now. For this first mindfulness meditation, we're going to keep things simple and direct. Meditation is, in the end, an incredibly simple activity. Essentially, you just sit and tune into what's going on. Let's do that right now.

There's no need to get ready in any special way. However, it's best if you are alone in a quiet, undisturbed place. Turn off all phones, messaging, and other distractions. You can either do it by reading it here, or accessing it as a guided meditation audio online at themindfulgeek.net. Ready? Let's go.

FIRST PRACTICE

Sit down. Find a posture that feels firm and stable. You can sit in a chair or on the floor.

Next, sit up straight.

Now, relax your entire body. If you want to, you can take a few deep breaths, letting them out with a sigh.

Now you're ready to begin your first mindfulness practice.

Allow yourself to become aware of the sensations in your feet. Tune into whatever feelings you're having there.

As you contact these sensations, say the word, "Feel" to yourself. Quietly in your mind. "Feel" is the label to use for body sensations.

Explore the sensations in your feet with curiosity and openness. How does it feel? If it's pleasant, enjoy that. If it's unpleasant, try to relax and accept that.

Next feel the sensations in your hands. Feel whatever is going on in your hands with as much curiosity and openness as you can.

Remember that there is no particular way you're supposed to feel. There may be pleasant feelings, unpleasant feelings, neutral feelings, or a mixture of them. You may notice a lot of mental talk. All of this is fine, just accept whatever's coming up.

Continue this for as long as you like, feeling sensations anywhere else in your body. (I recommend at least 5-10 minutes.)

When it's time to finish, spend a few moments just sitting quietly.

Small Steps

Congratulations, You've taken your first step into a larger world. You are now a mindfulness meditator. By sitting down and doing the practice, you've made it through the first rite of passage. Even if that one, simple technique is all you ever do, it will give you good results if you repeat it often.

Remember that mindfulness meditation is not about attempting to create a particular state of mind or body. If you are tense or in pain (and there's nothing you can do about it currently), then just allow that to happen and accept it. If you feel a rush of "energy" (in the sense of feeling like taking action) or strong pleasure, don't try to make that stronger. Just notice and accept it. You're cultivating an attitude of awareness and acceptance only. However, if you're not feeling particularly accepting, that's OK, too. Accept that you can't accept it. And the flipside is important, too: if you find that you are judging things that happen in the meditation, try not to judge yourself for judging. To the best of your ability, just accept that you are feeling judgmental right now. All this being OK with not being OK may sound silly at first, but the more you practice, the more you become aware of your mental processes, the more these paradoxes will start to make sense.

Although it's certainly possible, it's not likely that you contacted the contents of your deep unconscious during this first sit. You may be incensed that it didn't work to "make the unconscious conscious," like I said it would. You may be ready to demand your money back.

Not all insights are huge or significant, however. For example, did you notice anything at all about yourself or your experience that you hadn't noticed before? Many people in their first meditation come into direct contact with the fact that they have a very hard time sitting still. That is an insight. Or you may have noticed that your mind was constantly spinning the whole time. That's another insight. You may have noticed that you have an awful pain in your back that you hadn't felt previously. You guessed it: another insight.

Other insights may be more personal. For example, you may have noticed something in your environment for the first time and had a feeling of like or dislike for it. Perhaps there's a plant near you that you had never paid attention to, and now you realize that you actually think it's beautiful. Even that is an aspect of insight, making the unconscious conscious, the unknown known. In little ways, meditation is already doing the trick, already delivering at least a modicum of insight.

These insights may be utterly quotidian at this point, or they may not. Not every insight will be earth-shattering. Many of them are mundane, but as a group, as a body of knowledge, they slowly add up to something useful. You begin, as it is said, to "know thyself." Not only the Greek Oracle at Delphi, but psychology and neuroscience agree that *that* is a powerful thing.

The Shocking Truth

I like science experiments, especially ones that deal with meditation and neuroscience. Some experiments, however, are better than others, and some are just plain wonderful. The research study that is my current favorite asked the question: Would you rather sit alone with your thoughts or get a painful electric shock? The answer seems so obvious, and the obvious answer is so wrong.

Researchers at the University of Virginia and Harvard wanted to test[40] how happy people are while sitting alone and thinking. They placed hundreds of volunteers in sparsely furnished rooms for "thinking periods" of between 6-15 minutes in duration. Subjects were not allowed to touch their smartphones or other items. There were no games, no movies, no entertainment, or distractions. They were supposed to just think. When questioned afterwards about the quality of their experience, the volunteers were very clear: They did not like it. Even when the researchers next allowed them to sit in their own homes, or outdoors, and just think, they still didn't like it.

They reported that they liked reading or listening to music twice as much as just thinking.

This is where the study took a fascinating turn. The researchers were so surprised at how much the subjects disliked sitting alone with their thoughts, that they devised an almost-evil-but-actually-beautiful stratagem. The kind of thing that makes me love science.

They created a new "thinking room," and provided subjects with just one distraction: the ability to give themselves a painful electric shock. Either just hang out and think, or electrocute yourself. What do you suppose happened? Before you answer, consider the fact that all the participants had previously stated that they would *pay good money* to avoid an electric shock. There were no subjects who thought getting shocked was their idea of a good time. They had one job: sit in an empty room with their own thoughts for fifteen minutes, and *not* hurt themselves.

But it was too much for a lot of people. Twenty-five percent of women, and a walloping 67 percent of men chose to self-administer a painful electric shock, rather than sit there quietly with their thoughts. The researchers explained the difference between men and women by saying that men are "more sensation seeking." I'll say. One guy (who wasn't included in the final study) liked the shocks so much that he did it 190 times in the 15 minutes.

The point here is that it's not easy for people to sit quietly swimming around in the contents of their own heads. There are many possible reasons for this, although the first one you might think of—that they can no longer get along without the Internet, and that we've gotten so device-centric that we are slaves to our smartphones—seems to be false. Participants were aged 18-77, and the older folks presumably are not suffering from Internet addiction or a brain formed within a culture of continuous video game gratification. So this auto-electrocution doesn't represent a modern penchant for technological distractions. A more likely guess is that we, along with all mammals, evolved to explore our environment and continuously scan for new threats and opportunities. The brain just likes to be busy.

How does this relate to meditation? Well, you may have discovered that sitting and doing the meditation was about as fun as being shocked with a nine volt battery. While most people like mindfulness right away, in my experience, a decent percentage of students find their first sit (remember "to sit" in this context means "to meditate") uncomfortable or slightly unpleasant. A small number even find it really unpleasant, at first. Almost always, this is related to the feelings of the subjects in the above experiment: beginner meditators sometimes have a really hard time sitting with the activity of their own minds.

But even if you had a tough time sitting, there's hope. Because in this form of meditation, you're not actually just letting your mind wander. Instead, you are directing your mind toward contacting your body sensations. It's a structured mental investigation of your own sensory experience, not just a time of free-association and mind-wandering. As the researchers say in the paper: "This [difficulty controlling the mind] may be why many people seek to gain better control of their thoughts with meditation and other techniques, with clear benefits... Without such training, people prefer doing to thinking, even if what they are doing is so unpleasant that they would normally pay to avoid it. The untutored mind does not like to be alone with itself."

One of the authors of the electric shock study, Dan Gilbert, together with Matthew Killingsworth, both of Harvard, conducted another piece of research that reveals a startling fact about the human brain.[41] They wanted to determine how mind-wandering correlated with emotional tone. They achieved this by doing what any good geeks would do: they created a mobile smartphone app that would contact people at random intervals throughout their normal daily lives and ask them several questions: (1) what they were doing, (2) how happy they felt (from 1-100), and (3) whether they were focusing on what they were doing or not. If not, was what they were thinking about pleasant, unpleasant, or neutral? Response to the experiment was unusually large, and soon Gilbert and Killingsworth had assembled a database of over a quarter of a million samples from over 5000 people of all ages and from 83 countries.

The results were fascinating. It turns out that it doesn't matter much what activity a person is doing. Typically fun activities didn't correlate much with happiness. Instead, what matters is whether you are paying attention to what you are doing. Focused attention was strongly correlated with feeling happy, whereas having a wandering mind was usually accompanied by unpleasant feelings. Interestingly, human beings are very prone to mind wandering. It occurred in nearly 50 percent of all samples.

In short, the human mind is a wandering mind, and a wandering mind is an unhappy mind. There are many ways of feeling better, but one of the most powerful is simply to *concentrate on what you are doing in the moment*. Concentrating on what you are doing is, of course, the essence of mindfulness practice. As you sit more and more, you'll probably notice that you're feeling better more often.

So now you've had an experience of mindfulness meditation. With that, we can begin to unpack the nuances of the practice, introduce you to some new techniques, and dig deeper into the heart of the matter.

As you're reading the rest of this book, I encourage you to do mindfulness meditation at least once every day for five to ten minutes. That will keep you engaged in the practice, and you'll begin accruing some of the benefits. And, importantly, it will keep your head inside the work we're doing here. It will help you to enjoy and understand the nerdy shop talk we're going to dive deeply into. Planet Meditation, here we come.

CHAPTER FOUR

Labeling

In his seminal cyberpunk novel *True Names* (1981), Vernor Vinge postulated a world-spanning Internet, in which a new breed of computer hackers—called "warlocks"—vie for power in the real world. Using virtual reality gear to navigate the "Other Plane," they perpetrate ever-more dramatic pranks and heists, all the while jealously guarding their most precious secret: their true names. The anonymity of their avatars allows them to escape any sort of justice, but if another warlock acquires a real name, then they are at that warlock's mercy. They must work for him or her, or risk being revealed to the authorities in real life and suffering the consequences.

The idea of the power of the "true name" resembles an ancient magical principle—a fact that Vinge exploits for maximum dramatic effect. If you know something's true name, the belief goes, then you completely control it. That's how sorcerers bind demons to their will. Something similar exists in mindfulness meditation, and it's the practice of labeling. By giving a name to your experience, you can begin to get a handle on it, a new ability to understand and cope with it.

In our first meditation practice, I asked you to label your body sensations as "feel." Since most people think that meditation is about clearing your mind of thoughts, it may seem odd that I'm asking you to essentially create labeling thoughts. Why clutter the mind with more noise?

First, remember that meditation is *not* about clearing your mind of thoughts. Second, labeling is a great ally in meditation and is a standard feature of mindfulness practice. Distracted thoughts pull your attention away from the object of your meditation, but labeling helps to focus your attention on it. So even though you're technically creating extra words in your head, these words are helping you to remain mindful.

The labels also tend to fill up the mental talk channel with calm, neutral words, rather than agitated, unpleasant words, which also enhances the effects of meditation. There is some interesting research evidence that suggests that the process of labeling in meditation (particularly labeling affect, or feeling tone) increases the potency of mindfulness's beneficial effects.[42]

Labeling means giving a name to sensory experience that you have noticed. Mindfulness is the act of noticing sensory experiences, and each time you do this, you can make a label to help you focus on that experience. Thus, the basic instructions are:

1. Notice something
2. Label it
3. Go to 1

That's it. Like most technologies, however, there are some well-understood failure modes to labeling. Let's look at how to label correctly and how to avoid the most common pitfalls.

Be Gentle — When you "speak" a mental label, it should be very soft sounding. Like you're whispering sweet nothings to a baby. Don't be loud, harsh, anxious, or stern sounding. Allow all your labeling to be soothing. Do it in a relaxed and open manner.

Don't Try Too Hard — You will not get in trouble if you miss labeling a few sensory events. There is no Big Spreadsheet in the Sky keeping track of if you miss something. You will not go to Meditation Hell. Just relax and label what you comfortably can without getting too wound up or stressed out about it.

You Don't Have to Be Right — In some meditation techniques, you will have two or more labels, and the task involving distinguishing between different types of sensory experiences. Under these conditions, people often worry that they're labeling the events "wrong," that they're distinguishing them incorrectly. That's OK! See the above suggestion. Guessing and not-knowing are fine.

It's not a Mantra — You create a label each time you notice the thing that you are meditating on. It's literally *naming* the object you've noticed. That means that you don't want to just be making mental labels mechanically, in the mode of a mantra, with no object for them to refer to. Each label names a specific object (or objects) you've noticed. In a way, it's like adding metadata tags to each sensory event that you notice.

Slowly, Slowly — It's possible that sometimes you might be meditating on a type of sensory experience that is very active. For some people there can be very busy sensory experiences with a tremendous number of sensory events firing off in rapid sequence. The urge under these conditions can sometimes be to start labeling at high speed, in an attempt to name each and every sensation. They end up like the meditation equivalent of Lucy in the Chocolate Factory.[43]

But meditation shouldn't be speedy and frantic like that. Instead, allow a single label to count for several instances of similar objects arising. Keep the speed down to something like one label every few seconds. More than that can feel too busy and disrupt the focusing effect of the labeling.

Always Optional — Labeling is there to help you meditate more effectively. If, for whatever reason, labeling is annoying, too hard, makes you feel too wired, or is otherwise not helpful, then drop it. Don't let yourself get frustrated or bugged by the practice. Only use it if it's useful to you.

These hints should keep you out of the weeds. People typically find labeling a little unusual at first, but settle into it after a few sessions. Additionally, there are some useful variations you might try. The point of labeling is to help you focus, and these options exist to give you extra assistance when you're having trouble focusing.

Spoken Labels — If you're meditating alone, and you like to add some industrial-strength oomph to your concentration, you can speak the labels aloud. You will be surprised how hard it is to lose your focus when you're doing this.

Multiple Labels, or "Re-noting" — Sometimes sensory experiences are arising slowly, and there seems to be a lot of time in-between labels. Under these conditions, it's possible that your attention will drift while waiting for the next arising. To combat this, you can speak more than one label per sensory event. While this seems to contradict what I said under "It's not a mantra," it actually doesn't. You're still labeling an event, just more than once.

The labels you learn in this book are fairly standard, but you don't have to stick with them. For example, instead of the label "feel," for body sensation, you might like the label "body." Fine, use that instead. Make labeling work for you.

CHAPTER FIVE

Getting It Right

Albert Einstein once said, "a person who never made a mistake never tried anything new." It's actually pretty hard to make a mistake in meditation, but maybe the biggest challenge that beginning meditators encounter is the often mistaken belief that they're *doing it wrong*. I'm not sure of the reason for this—maybe it's just a quirk of our culture—but in my teaching experience it certainly comes up a lot. People just get *convinced* that they're practicing meditation incorrectly. Maybe it's because their thoughts aren't stopping and they're not suffused with infinite bliss?

From what I've seen, virtually everybody who thinks that they're doing it incorrectly is actually doing it right. While it may take time to get really good at it, most of meditation is just making the effort to sit each day. Do that and the practice will work its magic on you over time.

Still positive that you're screwing up? OK, let's go over the common ways that people actually *can* get it wrong. If you happen to have stumbled into one of these pitfalls, they are easy to climb out of.

The most common mistake, and the most ironic, is getting *caught up in the idea that you're messing it up*. The only way you're making a mistake here is that you're not concentrating on your meditation object, but instead directing all your attention toward beating yourself up. The solution is simple, let go of your fixation with how you're messing it up, and voilà, you're not messing up anymore.

A second problem is letting yourself become *grossly distracted*. It's possible to sit as if meditating, but allow yourself to get lost in endless fantasizing. Dreams of delicious meals, mind blowing sex with forbidden partners, or the remote island you want to transform into a nation state/pirate haven/Bond villain lair can seem a lot more interesting than focusing on the bodily sensations of your big toe. So, if you're fantasizing on purpose, and not even trying to concentrate on meditating, that's a problem. The solution is simple: Stop that! Start trying to concentrate.

Fantasizing on purpose is different from just getting distracted, which is totally normal and not a problem. Having a wandering mind isn't a crime against nature. It's just part of being a meatbot guided by a meatbrain. Let go of any self-recrimination, don't beat yourself up, and gently shift your attention back to the focus object.

The third common problem is *falling asleep*. That's not a bad thing, but it's not meditating. You might need the sleep. Most of us are chronically overworked and don't get enough rest. By all means, get all the deep, delicious sleep you require. But sleeping is not meditating. Although relaxation is helpful, you're not trying to get so relaxed that you conk out. There's a reason that Buddhist monks are sometimes credited with the invention of caffeinated tea. When it's time to meditate, wake up and pay attention to your focus object.

A fourth common problem is *trying too hard*. Some percentage of people takes a heroic, overachieving attitude toward their practice. They try to concentrate as hard as they can, and to have ultra-sharp sensory clarity at every moment, never missing a scintilla of what's happening.

This can be a good thing—a passion to learn is excellent—but beyond a certain level it's self-defeating. All the stress you produce from trying so hard is undoing the positive effects of the meditation. Remember that acceptance is a key element of meditation, and a big part of acceptance is relaxation. Try hard, but stay loose and open.

A fifth common problem is *stopping the meditation before you're finished*. Usually this happens because you just can't stand to sit anymore. You feel too upset, anxious, busy, distracted, or bored to keep going, and so you give up before the timer rings. It's good that you're meditating at all, so don't beat yourself up too violently over stopping. In the long run, however, it's best if you can overcome these urges and are able to stay meditating no matter what.

The secret to being able to stay sitting when you feel like you just can't stay sitting is this: meditate on the reaction that's trying to catapult you out of your seat. That is, if you're feeling upset, see if you can find where that upset is manifesting in your body. It might be a strong feeling of tension in your belly, or a sharp tightness in your throat. Focus your awareness on that spot, investigating it in detail. At the same time, try to be as accepting of it as possible. With practice, meditating on the reaction to the meditation can significantly deepen your meditation, as well as keep you seated for the allotted time.

The last common problem is a little subtler: *entertaining yourself with a slew of different meditation techniques*. Maybe you learned mantra meditation at some point in your life, and then experimented with self-inquiry for a while, but these days you are all about basic mindfulness. Now when you feel bored with meditation, you switch from one technique to another to another. While that can be entertaining, it means that you're not achieving deep contact with your focus object. Instead, you're ping-ponging around to keep yourself amused.

That kind of practice pinball doesn't allow you to get the maximum benefit from your meditation. It's closely related to rank fantasizing. So decide which practice you're going to do during your session, and for how long, and stick with it for the entire session. If you want to switch techniques in different sessions, that's fine, but don't give in to the urge to jump from technique to technique in a single session.

If you're avoiding these pitfalls, then you're doing meditation right. Sometimes practice is uncomfortable (even painful), sometimes quite boring, and sometimes it's filled with a lot of thinking. That's all fine. The thing to do as a mindfulness practitioner is simply (even if it's hard) bringing a lot of acceptance to these difficult experiences, as you are able, and to keep going.

While it may take time to get good at meditation, it takes almost no time to be able to follow the instructions properly. Thus, rest assured that *you are probably doing it right.*

Posture

Another important feature in getting it right is sitting well. In order to meditate, it helps to sit with your back upright. You don't want to go to sleep during meditation. When the spine is erect, it signals the central nervous system to be more alert. Remember, meditation means to make the unconscious conscious. Falling asleep is the opposite of that: you're going from conscious to unconscious. So, it's desirable to stay awake during meditation, and sitting up will help you to do that.

Beyond that one condition, I don't recommend worrying about your posture. You can sit in a chair, sit on the floor, or sit on a specially made meditation pillow or bench. In my experience, whatever works is fine. All that matters for the practice is that you're comfortable and have an erect spine.

Some traditional schools put a lot of emphasis on correct meditation posture, and different schools give different postures as the right one. My experience is that good posture is useful. There are some interesting effects of posture on psychology. For example, one study found that both men and women experience important neuroendocrine and behavioral changes merely by adopting a high-power posture (open, expansive) rather than a low-power (closed, contractive) one. There were significant increases in testosterone (in both sexes), lowering of cortisol, and increased feelings of power. So the postures you take may have an effect on your biology and psychology.[44] I'm unaware of any studies that specifically look at the changes brought about by meditation postures, but sitting in a relaxed, alert, somewhat composed manner seems to have a positive effect on the practice.

Beyond that, being as comfortable as possible is important. Once you're sitting in your meditation posture, refrain from outright fidgeting. I remember my first (and second and third) attempts at meditation. I was extremely excited about doing it, and was convinced that I'd get enlightened within a year, tops. I had a ridiculously naive and idealistic image about the practice, and thought that "real meditators" sat in full lotus posture for hours on end, completely motionless, experiencing ecstatic bliss without a trace of thoughts in their heads.. Imagine how frustrated I was when I found that I couldn't even stay still for a few minutes, let alone the fact that my brain felt like it was a tennis ball bouncing around the inside of my skull and my knees were screaming in agony.

I can relate to the challenges of beginning a meditation practice. I would say that if you're meditating for only 10 minutes, there's really no reason—short of some sort of physical injury that's causing pain—to move around much once you get your posture right. Any movements you're making are typically the result of anxiety and nervous agitation.

What's the big deal with sitting still? Just like having an agitated mind makes you fidgety, having an antsy body stirs the mind. Remaining physically still creates a feedback loop with your mind and allows your thoughts to settle down. There are other factors as well, such as the fact that it's much easier to meditate on subtle body sensations when you're not moving around.

While it may be difficult or uncomfortable at first, try your best to resist the urge to fidget about. If you cannot help it, and it would make the difference between sitting and not sitting, then by all means sit and fidget. It's not a deal breaker. My own fidgeting took years to subside, but it finally did. Eventually, if you stick to your practice, the nervous agitation will mellow out, and you'll be able to sit calmly.

CHAPTER SIX

The Three Elements

Now that you've actually meditated, it's time to learn a little meditation theory. If we were in computer coding class, you would've just completed your first "Hello, World!" program. Now would be the time to teach you the concept of MVC. That's the idea that the architectural pattern for any software containing a user interface can best be implemented using three separate but interconnected pieces: model, view, and controller. A lot of software that has a user interface uses some version of this pattern.

In meditation class, we also begin with a concept of three separate but interconnected pieces: concentration, sensory clarity, and acceptance (CCA). No matter what meditation technique you're using, it will probably be composed of some ratio of these three core elements.

Concentration means being able to train your attention on whatever object you choose, and sustain it there over time.

Sensory clarity means having a lot of resolution of the details of whatever object you're focusing on.

Acceptance means having an attitude of openness, curiosity, and nonjudgment with whatever is happening in the moment.

The three of them interact to make meditation deeper, more powerful, and more effective. In a typical mindfulness meditation, you're focusing on a body sensation (concentration), working to make fine distinctions about various qualities of that sensation (sensory clarity), and maintaining an attitude of openness and nonjudgment about the sensation (acceptance).

If even one of these elements is a little bit present, you can have a decent meditation. For example, let's say you just can't feel any acceptance about a particular painful body sensation. You feel upset about it, like you don't deserve to be having this sensation. Furthermore, this emotional upset is causing you to lose all sensory clarity. It just feels bad, and that's all you can tell about it. But painful sensations are helpful in one way, and that's that they are easy to concentrate on. Even if you tried hard to focus on something else, a painful sensation is hard to ignore. Thus it's easy in this case to concentrate, and in that way, to have a fairly good meditation experience. Even if two of the three elements are almost (but not entirely) missing, the healthy presence of the third one will save the day.

It works the same way with the other two. Sometimes you cannot focus or get any clarity, but will feel a good amount of acceptance. That can be a decent meditation. Other times, you experience a lot of sensory clarity, but your attention is flittering around and you don't feel much acceptance. Again, this can be a good meditation, too.

If two or three of the elements are strong, then your meditation experience will usually be quite good. Developing all three is the key to strengthening and deepening your meditation practice. Let's look at each of these elements in more detail.

Concentration

For many people, the words "concentration" and "meditation" mean the same thing. And it's true that being able to concentrate is an important meditative skill. Concentration, or focus, means that you can direct your attention to the object you choose, and hold it there. The better your concentration, the longer you can hold it without interruption.

In the beginning, however, even directing your attention for more than a few moments can be challenging. For most people without training, attention is difficult to control—like Luke trying to use the Force to drag his X-wing out of a Dagobah swamp. You want to focus on your homework, but the television grabs your eyeballs. The page you're reading is right in front of you, but you're so lost in thought about your partner's bodily charms that you can't even process the words. It seems that your brain doesn't even belong to you, that you can't control it. It's as if you turned the wheel of your car left and instead it went right. You're trying to go to the grocery store, but your car wants to go to the gas station, so it just overrides you and does whatever it wants. That is the condition of most people's attention, most of the time. Attention seems to be an unruly servant, at best. Whose brain is it, anyway?

Because meditation deals directly with the attention, when you first begin sitting, you may get a real shock about the condition of your powers of concentration. It becomes immediately apparent that you're not in control of your own mind. There are valid, neuroscientific reasons for this, mainly that it's completely unclear whether we're in conscious control of anything, but that's a topic for another book.[45]

On top of that, most of the targets of mindfulness meditation are things that you probably have never paid very much attention to before in your life. Focusing on them usually seems almost comically boring, useless, narcissistic, or quotidian. We are just not used to giving a lot of attention to the minute sensations in our feet, for example. It just feels weird and difficult. Most of us do not have a lot of neural resources allocated to tasks like this.

Concentrating on body sensations may feel difficult to do, and your attention will kind of slide away from the object over and over again. It will almost magnetically be drawn to things that you normally pay attention to, such as your smartphone apps or a favorite TV show. You've probably spent a lot more time noticing these things than the sensory experiences of your right big toe.

It's natural and even healthy that, in the beginning, your attention is going to be captured by things that are not your meditation object. ("Meditation object" or "focus object" are the clunky-but-concise phrases I'll use to mean the thing you're supposed to be focusing on.)

The solution is simple: *brute force repetition*. Each time your attention is drawn away from the meditation object, gently bring it back. Over and over, notice that your focus has wandered and return it to the chosen object. Each one of these returns can be thought of as a concentration "rep," just like a weightlifting "rep" at the gym. With each weightlifting rep, your muscles are growing stronger. In the same way, with each concentration rep your concentration grows stronger. Luckily, concentration is a trainable skill, so it just keeps getting more buff as you iterate your reps. Bulking up your focus power is one of the most widely demonstrated benefits of meditation[46] practice.

We can model concentration as a kind of extremely simple algorithm:

1. Place attention on the focus object.
2. Check if attention has wandered.
3. If no, continue. If yes, then 1.

Iterating through this algorithm not only creates focus as you're doing it, it permanently builds your concentration "muscle," your focus power. Iterating through this a large number of times (something like 10^6 or 10^7) will build immense concentration that can stay on a single object for a very long time. So this sort of iteration increases the time dimension of your concentration. Your attention span gets huge.[47]

The good news is that your attention span doesn't just become longer during meditation practice, it becomes longer for all the other activities of your life. You can do better at school work, work projects, or anything else you want to devote attention to. Even a two-week course in mindfulness meditation has been shown to increase working memory and GRE performance.[48] Gaining the ability to focus on anything you want to, for as long as you want, is one of the most powerful ways the mindfulness meditation can improve your life.

Sensory Clarity

"That's no moon. It's a space station." ~ Obi-Wan Kenobi

Meditation is a kind of awareness-extending technology, like a telescope or a microscope. When you begin the practice of mindfulness, you are training your awareness on present-moment sensory experiences. At first this will feel pretty normal. But after while, you'll be able to greatly increase your ability to detect finer and finer qualities of sensation at ever smaller scales. Your brain just gets better at detecting the sensations in finer and finer areas of the body. This aspect of meditation is called "sensory clarity," where you use your awareness like a telescope or microscope to "see" subtler sensory experiences. Sensory clarity takes a while to develop and requires that you attempt to make ever-finer sensory distinctions in your meditation practice.

For example, if I asked you to concentrate on the bodily sensations currently present in your right hand, what would you feel? Most people with no meditation experience typically report feeling their entire hand. It's as if the sensations in the hand can only be experienced as one big pixel of information. Or maybe they have a little bit of sensory clarity—we could also call it sensory "resolution"—and they can feel, say, 4 or 9 big pixels of feeling data in their hand. With practice, the resolution of sensory data becomes much higher, say 128 pixels. Eventually, you will be able to effortlessly detect pixels as small as a grain of salt, everywhere in the hand.[49] One study found that meditators were not only able to focus much better than controls (after only four days of intensive practice), but that they increased "the depth of information processing" as well.[50] Another study focusing on tactile sensations looked at a number of objective and subjective measures of "sensitivity" in experienced meditators—for example, the measured area of the cortex dedicated to tactile sensation.[51] Here researchers found that meditation "enhances introspective accuracy for bodily sensations," meaning that practitioners really do have greater sensory clarity than non-meditators.

You may very well ask why in the hell would anybody want to develop that? How could such ability possibly improve your life? As I mentioned in the introduction, I won't ask you to do anything that won't obviously and relatively quickly improve your life. Here's how sensory clarity will help to do this.

Let's say you're taking a nice warm shower in the morning. Let's further assume that you really love taking warm showers. In the "big pixel," low-resolution version you begin with, that nice experience is kind of hard to get a hold of. It's just one fuzzy unfocused lump of awareness. Because it's low-resolution, it takes up very little of your available attention and thus you're having a lot of other thoughts and feelings while your shower is happening. These can detract from your pleasure to a large degree, especially if you're anxious on this particular morning, and your head is filled with thoughts of the workday. That one big fuzzy pixel of good feeling in your body has a hard time competing for attention with all that worry.

If, however, you've developed a bit of sensory clarity, something different happens. Let's say you've worked for a year on your mindfulness meditation practice, and you've developed a walloping 128 pixels of sensory clarity anywhere on your body. Then, when the warm, soothing shower water hits any part of your body, you can experience it with startling resolution and depth. Each pixel feels good in its own way, so the experience is much richer and more rewarding. Secondly, it takes up much more room in awareness—hogs more of the RAM in your working memory—and so pushes out extraneous thoughts and feelings. There's far less room in your mind for anxiety about the day, for example. So the whole experience of the warm shower goes from something that's "nice" to an all-consuming experience of quasi-orgasmic pleasure all over.

If you think that I'm exaggerating the power of sensory clarity, I invite you to try the practices in this book for a month. You will see for yourself that even a little sensory clarity can go a long way toward improving your life. What's great is that it's doing this without actually changing the external circumstances of your life in any way. It's the same shower as you were taking before, but now you're just enjoying it so much more. You're getting more bang for your buck, regardless of what pleasurable thing you're doing.

Sensory clarity is wonderful for other senses, too. Imagine gazing at your favorite works of art (or other beautiful objects) with eyes that have developed a high degree of visual resolution. It's like HD for your eyes, or listening to your favorite music with super-attuned hearing. Even your senses of taste and smell can vastly improve with sensory clarity.

Acceptance

The third of the three elements of meditation is acceptance.[52] Acceptance is extremely simple, much simpler than the other two. Just accept whatever your experience is, that's all. Acceptance means maintaining a radical hands-off policy with regards to your sensory experience. Acceptance means to not try to change it, to not try to control it, to not try to hang onto it, to not try to push it away, to not resist it. Mostly acceptance means to not judge your sensory experience.[53] The motto for acceptance is, "It is what it is."

It's important to notice that acceptance means accepting your sensory experience, not accepting the conditions of your life. You're free to take all the actions necessary or desirable to make your life better. Acceptance doesn't mean becoming passive or inactive. It just means that the current sensory experience is what it is, and you accept that part of things.

Acceptance will not only deepen your meditation practice considerably, it will also alter your life in other ways.[54] When you quit resisting everything all the time, things can become easier and more enjoyable for you very quickly.

I had a friend who loved a good view of nature. I remember standing with him in the mountains of Colorado, together, gazing upon one of the most stunning natural vistas I'd ever seen. I was just floored by how beautiful it was. Right in the middle of this moment, he said, "Those phone lines ruin the view." Looking around, I noticed that, way down in the valley, there were some telephone lines strung between the few homes there. I hadn't even noticed them, and yet these little phone lines were all that he noticed. The view might be nice, even magnificent, but in his view, it was wrecked by a minimal intrusion that he couldn't accept.

Most of us live in a state of perpetual "could be better." We're so used to having control over every little parameter of our lives that we cannot focus on what's going right, only on what's going wrong. That's the viewpoint we always seem to be coming from, and it means that we are perpetually unsatisfied, unhappy, disappointed, and ungrateful. These are not pleasant emotions to be constantly soaking in.

It's important to change what we can about our lives to make them better. On the other hand, in this moment, there is only what is happening now. In most (but not all) meditation practices, the idea is to accept what is happening in the moment.

Another metaphor for how the three elements work comes from a video screen. Concentration means you can direct your attention to any part of the screen you want. Sensory clarity is like switching the screen setting from low-res to HD. And acceptance is how the screen displays whatever signals it gets, without judging or controlling the content.

Each of the three elements of meditation—concentration, sensory clarity, and acceptance (CCA)— can almost function as a complete meditation on their own. That is, there are practices that strongly utilize only concentration, sensory clarity, or acceptance individually. Putting them all together in a single practice, however, each one of them tends to reinforce the others. In the next chapter on *The Meditation Algorithm*, you'll see my system for putting them together.

CHAPTER SEVEN

The Meditation Algorithm

When you did the first practice in this book, I had you contact and label your meditation object. But now that you know about CCA, the three elements of mindfulness meditation, it's time to learn how to bring those into your practice.

Just as concentration can be expressed as an algorithm, the process of mindfulness meditation can also be modeled as a repeated sequence of steps. This algorithm assumes that you've already sat down, relaxed, and gotten all set to meditate. It also assumes that you know which meditation technique you're going to practice.

Once you are ready to actually meditate, the practice is expressed by this algorithm:

1. Notice the focus object.
2. Label the focus object.
3. Allow awareness to deeply contact the focus object.
4. Feel acceptance toward whatever you find there.
5. Continue focusing, contacting, and accepting for about 5 seconds.
6. Repeat.

You then iterate through this algorithm for the duration of your meditation session, changing Step 6 when you're ready to finish.

Let's look at the steps one at a time and see what's going on here.

Steps 1 and 5 are both concentration steps. In *Step 5*, you are maintaining contact with the focus object, and in *Step 1*, you are returning attention (which may have wandered) to the focus object. You may recognize these two steps as the entirety of the Concentration Algorithm I gave earlier.

Step 2 introduces Labeling. As discussed earlier, in mindfulness meditation, you can use labeling to help you maintain focus. Normally, you say the label mentally, softly. If you're alone, and you need some extra help concentrating, you can say the label aloud, again very gently. Only say it once per iteration of the algorithm.

An example of a label is the word "relaxed." If you were meditating on relaxed body sensations, each time you contacted such a sensation, you would mentally repeat this label to yourself.

Step 3 is the sensory clarity step. When awareness deeply contacts the focus object, you begin to notice lots of details about it. You may, for example, notice the felt size of the object. Its felt location, shape, texture, and other qualities are all aspects which become clear with high-resolution sensory investigation.

Step 4 is the acceptance step. It's very important in meditation to relax the need to change and control things. When you contact the focus object, you may have a knee-jerk reaction of dislike, disgust, or irritation about it. Let's say you're contacting a body sensation, and you discover that it is a painful, unpleasant sensation. Your first reaction may be to hate it, fear it, or want to push it away. You may begin telling yourself all kinds of stories about how it's bad, wrong, scary, or whatever.

In this acceptance step, however, try the best that you can to just let go of that reactivity. See if you can just let whatever sensation is arising to arise, without judging it or trying to change it or getting worked up about it.

It's almost impossible to overemphasize the importance of this step. If you are concentrating on your focus object, but with each iteration of the algorithm you are judging, storytelling, negatively reacting, and freaking out about the focus object, you will still be building concentration (and that's good), but you will also be training yourself to be in a bad mood (and that's not good). That will sharply reduce the benefits you get from the practice, because amping up a negative, judgmental, reactive mood will obviously reduce your wellbeing.

Whenever I teach the acceptance step, inevitably a new student asks something like, "But why should I accept a painful sensation? Shouldn't I do whatever it takes to fix it? Is meditation just teaching me to be a brainless, passive consumer?" Well, no. You have 23.5 hours a day to express your true nature as a negative, judgmental, reactive freak. For the duration of your meditation practice, however—just 30 minutes or less a day—experiment with accepting whatever is arising. I promise that it won't short-circuit your Free Will (if that even exists)[55] or transmogrify you into a mindless zombie reporting to the *Soylent Green* rendering plant.

Maybe, just maybe, you will get a little bit of relief by letting things just be for a while. Imagining that you have to judge, change, and control everything all the time is really stressful. If you can't accept that for the moment, skip to the Acceptance chapter where we'll discuss it in more depth there.

In Step 5, you're combining everything at once. You're staying concentrated on the object, maintaining sensory clarity about the qualities of the object, and doing your best to regard the object with acceptance.

You do this step for perhaps a few seconds. By then, we'll assume your attention has wandered, the focus object has changed in some way, or it's just time for another round. Therefore, you move on to Step 6, and return to Step 1.

Congratulations, you've just completed one iteration of the mindfulness algorithm. At first it may seem a little mechanical and programmatic to go through steps, one by one, during meditation. Some people dislike this method, mainly because it is so, well, systematic. But I strongly recommend doing it this way, at least until it becomes second nature. It's like a pianist practicing scales. Maybe she started learning the piano because the beautiful music moved her soul. It may seem that practicing scales couldn't be further from that experience. Yet, if she wants to someday play soul-stirring music, practicing scales is a very reliable way to get there.

It's the same with the meditation algorithm. You've got to put in the time doing the tiny steps, to make sure you're getting the full benefit. Eventually, these steps will unfold all at once, like one big Step 5, and it will feel as if you've been doing it for your whole life, like you were born to meditate. And that, my friend, will feel good.

The Meditation Algorithm

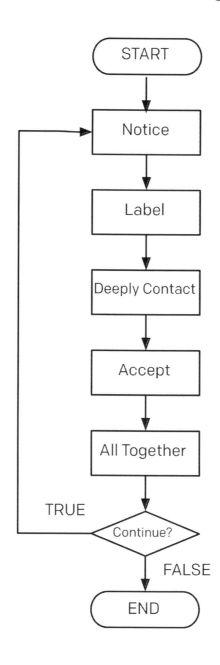

Using the Algorithm

Let's try a single round of the meditation algorithm now. It won't be a "real" meditation practice, so you can do this anywhere (except while operating heavy equipment or buying things online). As usual, we'll use the sensations arising in your hand as a focus object.

Find a place to sit and assume your meditation posture. Whether you're sitting in a chair, on a bench, on a cushion, or flat on the floor (yoga ninja!), make sure your spine is upright. Allow the rest of you to relax. Take a few deep breaths and release tension.

Once you're settled in, bring your attention to your left hand. Notice the feelings in your hand. As soon as you feel something, that's *Step 1*. You're noticing your focus object.

Step 2 is to label the sensation in your hand. In this case, use the label "hand." Very softly and gently, say the word "hand" to yourself in your mind.

Now that your attention is focused in the right place, pour your attention on the object. That is *Step 3*.

"Contacting it deeply" means to actively explore your focus object with a lot of curiosity. You definitely do not want to let Step 2 be the end of the process. Here, we're using the label as a *signal to dig more deeply* into the richness and depth of the experience. You want to get the sense that awareness is caressing, investigating, even permeating the focus object. Imagine that the sensations in your hand are a sponge, and that awareness is like water soaking into that sponge. It is "knowing" every bit of the sensations in your hand.

Alternately, you can imagine that all the nerves in your hand could be represented schematically as a tree structure. Step three means that your awareness contacts every node in that structure, feeling every nuance of the sensations in your hand. This is how you develop sensory clarity.

It may seem like it's possible to take this too far, and you may be tempted to just sort of ballpark it. I mean, pay attention to every little detail of sensation in your hand? Really? But the secret to success with sensory clarity is to take it too far, *take it way, way too far*. Get into every little micro detail of the sensations in your hand. The more you gently stretch yourself in the effort to investigate ever-subtler details of sensation, the more you're building the part of your brain (the insula) which allows you to feel your own body. It takes effort, but the effort is not wasted.

So really challenge yourself to dig into the details of sensation before moving on to Step 4. At a minimum, make sure you feel at least one very specific sensation somewhere in your hand.

Step 4 is about greeting whatever arises in your hand with acceptance. As I mentioned above, this is very important, but it doesn't have to be a big deal. Simply try to have a gentle, matter-of-fact quality about the sensations that appear there, even if they are unpleasant.

For example, let's say you have a small cut on your finger and it kind of aches a little. It's natural to be filled with lots of reactions: fear of infection, concern that something may be wrong with it, anxiety over whether to see a doctor, anger and shame that you hurt yourself ("I'm such an idiot!"), and a flaming sense of injustice that you got hurt at all.

These are normal reactions; don't try to fight them. Instead, attempt to find just a little bit of acceptance in yourself for this achy sensation. Acceptance doesn't mean you have to love it or want to have a baby with it. It just means to allow it to be there—a kind of "it is what it is" stance toward it. This not only applies when a sensation is unpleasant, but also when you start to get hooked on a seductive sensation.

If you're having trouble with Step 4, and lots of people do, just get meta about it, and accept the fact that you're having trouble with it. It'll start you down the right road.

In *Step 5*, you put them all together for a few seconds. You're directing attention onto the focus object with great concentration. You're noticing all its details and qualities with great sensory clarity. You're allowing whatever you find there to just be, with great acceptance. You experience the elements all together in a bucket, with eggs on top.

Then, after a few seconds, you start from the beginning again, maybe on exactly the same sensation.

Try doing this now. Go through each step in laborious, excruciating detail. Read up on each step again, if you have to. See if you can get a sense of how the meditation algorithm works. Take your time. When you're done, come back to this spot in the text.

Plug and Chug

Congratulations, you've just completed one iteration of the meditation algorithm. Only 719,999 to go and you'll be an expert meditator. Good luck.

Where did I get that outrageously large number? Well, they say that it takes 10K hours of practice to become an expert at something. (That "theory," put forth by writer Malcolm Gladwell, has been fairly well debunked, but let's just go with it as a ballpark.)[56] And I've said that one iteration of the meditation algorithm should take approximately five seconds. Thus:

10,000 hours x 360 (number of seconds in an hour) = 3,600,000 seconds.

3,600,000 seconds / 5 = 720,000 iterations to become an expert meditator.

Of course, I'm just kidding around with the exactitudes of the pseudomath. You'll begin getting benefits of meditation long before this. Maybe with as little as one hour of practice (360 iterations). But it does make an important point, which is that each round, each iteration, of the meditation algorithm, is really pretty easy. It's not that taxing, and it doesn't last that long. It may even be, or become, quite pleasurable over time. Meditation becomes something people tend to really enjoy after some time of practicing. And repetition like this is the way that neuroplasticity is activated.

So each meditation session is composed of sitting down and turning the crank on the meditation algorithm. Plug and chug. Why not try some of that now?

CHAPTER EIGHT

Darwin's Dharma

Perhaps you've encountered the famous proclamation that, "Nothing in biology makes sense except in the light of evolution."[57] This statement is almost literally true. Without the principles of natural selection, mutation, genetic drift, and other mechanisms, biology becomes little more than a practice of taxonomy—grouping plants and animals into various categories—and not even a very accurate one at that.[58] As an explanatory mechanism for the processes of life, evolution is the key that unlocks the entirety of the science, and without it, you're just crashing around in the dark.

Humans are animals that evolved from primates, and not only our physiology, but also our psychology cannot be understood properly without an underlying knowledge of evolutionary biology. Our brains didn't just pop into existence from the void, fully formed and ready to proclaim themselves the masters of creation—although we often act as if they did. I love the idea in *2001: A Space Odyssey* that aliens tampered with evolution and enhanced our brains. Maybe they weren't aliens at all, but our future selves, traveling back in time to push a vital wetware upgrade to our own progenitors. (That would be a neat trick.) But beyond the amusement derived from such outrageous speculation, these science fiction ideas don't really help us to improve our wellbeing in this life. Instead, we have to stick with the science, which includes neuroscience, psychology, and evolutionary biology.

Our brains evolved from the brains of earlier primates. In fact, the structures of our brains closely resemble those of our ancestors. Granted, our brains are three times heavier than a chimpanzee's, and we have far more neuronal interconnectivity, but the basic model is remarkably similar. Which makes sense, since they're our closest relatives. Furthermore, there are many structures in our brains that are fairly similar to those of even distant ancestors/relatives.

A fascinating example of this is the brain structure known as a "mushroom body." University of Arizona neuroscientists Nicholas Strausfeld and Gabriella Wolff recently analyzed the pattern of mushroom bodies in a variety of species—everything from insects to horseshoe crabs to flatworms—and found them to be strikingly similar. Not only are individual mushroom body neurons similar in a multitude of organisms, but their network organization and protein expression are virtually identical, too. For a long time, mushroom bodies have been known to be implicated in learning and memory, and this study suggests that everything from a fruit fly to a bat—even a human being—uses essentially the same basic neuronal mechanism to do this.

Human brains don't have mushroom bodies—we have a cortex instead—but the cortex seems to have evolved directly from mushroom bodies.[59] Analysis shows that this basic mechanism is approximately 600 million years old[60], and has been conserved in almost all creatures since then. So core aspects of our brain and nervous system can be traced back a very long time indeed. Sorry, O Master of Creation, your nervous system may be extraordinarily complex, but in its fundamentals it runs on the same principles as a snail.

Pushmi-Pullyu Life

The fundamental aspect of a nervous system, whether that of a snail, a fish, a parrot, or a human being, is that it functions as a *behavioral guidance system*. It orients you toward food, shelter, mates—things that help with survival—and away from predators, cliffs, and poisons— things that do you in. Even the lowly paramecium, a single-celled protozoan shaped like a football, exhibits these behaviors. It's covered with cilia that propel it toward food, and away from toxins— and it doesn't even possess what we would think of as a nervous system. It could be that this simple binary choice—toward good things, away from bad things—lies at the basis of all complex behavior.

In animals with nervous systems, this behavioral guidance is subjectively experienced as signals of pleasure and pain. It's not as if chocolate actually contains molecules of indescribable-deliciousness (placed there by elves living in a hollow tree, no doubt), it's that our tongues are biologically coded to perceive fats and sugars as important survival compounds. When the brain receives the message from the tongue that it has lovingly slithered over some of these molecules, a hard-wired pleasure sensation explodes in your mind. Evolution is telling you to continue eating that Snickers bar because fats and sugars used to be hard to find.

Similarly the point of a needle doesn't have crystals of pain-essence embedded in it. The nerves in your skin are wired to signal when tissue damage occurs, and this triggers a subjective pain experience in your mind. This helps you to avoid accidentally poking holes in yourself—which can be annoying and inconvenient—without being aware of it.

Even at this rudimentary level, the nervous system has an "opinion" about what is good and bad for your survival, and lets you know it in no uncertain terms. The biological wisdom[61] built into the nervous system is the result of millions of years of evolution—which things are pleasant and which cause pain are usually things that are survival-positive and survival-negative, respectively.[62] So the biological machine that you are has some deeply embedded wiring that pushes you toward life-enhancing things (fats and sugars are rich energy sources), and away from life-harming things (stepping on broken glass can cause health issues). Subjectively, you experience these behavioral "pushes" in the form of pleasure and pain. Recent research seems to indicate the core of this pleasure/pain learning system is centered in the structure known as the amygdala.[63]

Almost everybody likes pleasure and dislikes pain, but both have their advantages and disadvantages. It's possible for something to make you feel *too* good, which can lead to over-indulgence and destructive behavior. We can all think of a few illegal substances that do just that. And if you didn't have pain, you could break your leg and have no idea. Pain keeps you out of trouble, so to speak.

If you're having difficulty accepting this fact, let me introduce you to a young man by the name of Roberto S. He is one of seventeen individuals in the United States who literally cannot feel pain due to a genetic condition known as congenital insensitivity to pain with anhidrosis (CIPA). Roberto is constantly laughing and smiling and is unusually happy. His mother couldn't believe what a good baby he was, because he never cried about anything.

As he grew a bit older, however, it became clear that something was very wrong. If he played outside in the heat, he couldn't sweat, and would get heatstroke. He stopped eating altogether and had to have a tube inserted in his stomach. When he was two and a half, he broke his foot, and walked around on it for days, oblivious. Like other children, Roberto went through teething, but unlike other children he gnawed on his tongue and lips to the point of mutilation. "If you could imagine when you bite your tongue how bad it hurts. At one point, you couldn't even distinguish that his tongue was his tongue," his mother said.

Roberto had to have most of his teeth surgically removed for his own protection, which is also why his hands stay wrapped most of the time. Because he never feels fatigue, he is hyperactive, but because he never feels hungry, he despises eating. Roberto's entire family is on constant call, making sure he doesn't inadvertently injure himself. Without modern medicine and the 24-hour care of his family, his life would have been very short. Most kids with this disorder die by the age of three.[64] Living without the feedback mechanism of pain is deadly.[65]

Although it's an incredibly reductive model, seeing the function of the nervous system as essentially a binary pleasure/pain-based guidance system is quite clarifying. Merely because a human being has a much more complex-seeming experience of the world than, say, a scorpion, doesn't mean that we have outgrown the biological basis of our nervous system. "Approach good things/flee bad things" may in some sense describe the drives underlying our entire lives, albeit without much of the nuance that we experience.

Pleasure and Pain

In mindfulness meditation, the general stance is to attempt to accept and investigate all sensory experience, regardless of its hedonic tone. Unpleasant sensory experiences are greeted (at least in theory) just as readily as pleasurable ones. There are several good reasons to do this.

One is that it's hard to investigate experiences that you are avoiding, suppressing, or denying. Remember that we are trying to make the unconscious conscious, and painful sensations are one of the things that we tend to push out of consciousness as much as possible. By stopping the suppression of these experiences, we allow them to enter conscious awareness. Given that pain signals are just as valuable behaviorally as pleasure signals, this is in itself interesting and useful.

A second reason is related to the first—you can get large insights by looking into painful sensations (especially very minor ones). By getting a clear look at what you are typically suppressing and denying, you will often be surprised by the clarity of understanding you gain into your own behavior.

A third reason is that our avoidance of pain signals, and the underlying conviction we have that they are bad, actually makes them *worse*. In Western culture, at least, there is a belief that pain is somehow unfair, wrong, and unnatural, and thus we experience a lot of emotional discomfort around it. And emotional distress is known to make physical pain worse—a fact exploited by torturers worldwide.[66] If, for example, you combine a physical pain with an experience of humiliation, it makes the experience of physical pain markedly worse.

The good news is that the opposite is also true—positive emotional experiences can make physical pain much less intense—and we can use this fact to our advantage in meditation. By cultivating a stance of acceptance of and even curiosity about painful experiences, we reduce the emotional distress about them, and can often reduce the experience of suffering as a result.

In one study, participants had a thermal stimulation device strapped to the back of their leg, which was then heated to a temperature of 120 degrees.[67] I've had a similar device strapped to my wrist in a neuroscience lab before. It looks like a black plastic box with tubes for hot water coming in and out of it. The heat of the water can be precisely controlled. When the hot water flows, it hurts more than you'd think, delivering a sharp stinging sensation. Subjects in this study were zapped with the heat, then received four 20-minute sessions of mindfulness training, and then were zapped with the heat again. The results were significant. After the meditation training they reported a 40 percent reduction in the intensity of the pain, and a 57 percent reduction in the unpleasantness of the heat. You might think that they were just imagining this difference, but brain scans taken during the experiment confirmed that there were marked changes in several brain regions associated with pain regulation and processing.

In short, even a little meditation training can make pain a lot more tolerable. Another fine example of meditation enhancing your experience of life!

I hasten to add that this acceptance of painful sensations in meditation doesn't mean that I'm counseling you to somehow accept bad life situations. People leap to this absurd conclusion so often that I'm required to repeat this disclaimer. No, learning to have a little openness and acceptance of difficult sensations that arise during meditation doesn't somehow mean that you are required to accept your partner abusing you or your local police department beating you for a broken tail light. It simply means that cultivating a stance of relative acceptance in meditation has helpful effects on your general experience of wellbeing.

And what about pleasurable sensations? How should you encounter those in meditation? For one, you are encouraged to enjoy them to their fullest. You can do this deeply by using concentration (to focus on them specifically) and sensory clarity (to get into the fine details of the pleasure), and—as usual—by accepting whatever you experience.

I can hear your indulgent chuckle: "Hehe, yes, I'll certainly be good at accepting those pleasurable sensations, hehe." It sounds easy, but remember that acceptance isn't just allowing it or letting it in, it also means not holding onto it, and includes letting it go. Grasping onto (in an emotional sense) pleasurable sensations, and not wanting to let go of them or allow them to pass, is a way of not accepting sensations. The reason for this is that the emotional distress of attempting to cling to a pleasant sensation that is passing away dramatically reduces your ability both to investigate and enjoy that pleasure. If instead you take a stance of understanding that all good feelings pass eventually, you will experience much more satisfaction with that pleasure. It's not tainted by emotional distress. Acceptance of pleasure in this sense is actually almost as difficult as acceptance of pain.

While acceptance of both pleasure and pain as they arise takes effort and practice over a long period of time, it's worth all of the energy expended. In addition to the reasons listed above, there is another, even more compelling reason, which has everything to do with our goal of life-enhancement. As reductive as it may be, I think we can all agree that our future experience of life will be composed of a large number of positive and negative experiences, a wide variety of pleasurable and painful moments. What if, by learning to encounter these experiences with some measure of acceptance, you can actually alter the "math" on all of them a little in your favor? That is, what if you can suffer just a little bit less with each painful experience for the rest your life? What if you can have just a little more fulfillment with each pleasurable experience?

Even if your meditation practice teaches you to do this only a fraction of a percentage point with each arising of sensory experience, the sheer number of them accruing, year after year, decade upon decade, could add up to quite a large difference in your subjective enjoyment of your own life. Given the absolute, crushing, undeniable inevitability of the fact of life—that various good and bad things will happen, both within and without your control—using your meditation practice to tip the experiential scales a bit in your favor only makes good sense.

Trying to accept both pleasure and pain in meditation is just one aspect of your practice that can be enhanced and understood more deeply in the light of evolutionary biology. We'll see more examples of this, beginning with the next chapter.

"Nature has placed mankind under the governance of two sovereign masters, pain and pleasure."~ Jeremy Bentham

CHAPTER NINE

Stress and Relaxation

When I first started teaching meditation, I thought that nothing could be easier than asking students to relax. Who wouldn't like that? Boy, did my students teach me differently. Asking them to relax elicited a variety of negative responses. Some people got upset, anxious, or angry in feeling that they were doing it wrong. Others noticed that they were not relaxed, and got really freaked out by how stressed they actually felt. And still others felt that they just couldn't relax, no matter how hard they tried. Sometimes the response I got was basically, "You want me to *relax?!* Fuck you!"

Maybe I'd just forgotten all my years of struggling to meditate, but I have to admit I was a little shocked by these responses. I mean, what feels better than relaxing? I had expected all my students to just love it (and most did). But the more I thought about it, the more the negative reactions of the few made sense. We Americans are not just stressed out, we are *chronically* stressed out. We've been stressed out *continuously for years*. We've gotten used to it. It's the norm. Being stuck in a pattern, even a painful, negative pattern, can be very difficult to let go of.

It's no secret that our lives are overly complicated, and becoming more so every day. The number of things we expect ourselves to accomplish in 24 hours has skyrocketed, as has a general intolerance for quiet, reflective activities such as sitting at home and reading. (Remember the study that shows that many people would rather electrically shock themselves than be alone with their thoughts?) And moments that in the past would've been quiet and relaxing have recently been filled with a plethora of bleeping, winking, and flashing technological distractions. Dangerous activities such as texting while driving are rampant. We are trying to do too much, too fast, all at once, and are living in a state of chronic stress as a result.

Stress activates a part of the neuroendocrine system called the *hypothalamic-pituitary-adrenal* (HPA) system. The HPA system (also known as the "stress axis") is thought to have evolved in the earliest vertebrates, and been maintained by evolution in all subsequent species, due to its extraordinarily important role in survival. Thus the stress hormones of reptiles, fish, and birds are similar to those in a human being.[68]

The HPA system evolved to cope with immediate survival threats. Let's say that you are an ancient proto-human, out gathering some roots in the field. Suddenly, you spot a large tiger coming at you. Your bodymind system goes into a very powerful sequential reaction to deal with this threat. This is called the "stress response." First, the HPA system manufactures and releases steroid hormones, called *glucocorticoids*, including the main stress hormone, *cortisol*. Cortisol is a crucial chemical for arousing the body to deal with danger (to run away from the tiger that you've spotted). It activates the heart, lungs, circulation, metabolism, immune systems, and skin, and prepares them to help you run away as fast as you can.

The HPA system also releases neurotransmitters called *catecholamines*, particularly dopamine, norepinephrine, and adrenaline. Catecholamines suppress the activity of the frontal lobes of your brain, making simple decision-making easier (fight or flight, anyone?), but hindering social interaction and complex task solving. They also trigger the amygdala—an area of the brain associated with an emotional response, usually fear—to have an appropriate response.

These neurotransmitters then signal the hippocampus to store the fear and other data about the experience in long-term memory so that you know how to survive a tiger attack next time, if you survive.[69]

The stress response then begins to change your body in amazing ways. Your blood flow increases as much as 400 percent, preparing the muscles, brain, and lungs for the ordeal. The spleen discharges white and red blood cells, enhancing the ability of the lungs to transport oxygen, and the rate of breathing speeds up to deliver this needed oxygen. The steroids released by the HPA dampen the immune system in order to redistribute immune molecules where they will most likely be needed: the skin, bone marrow, and lymph nodes. Fluids, which may be needed to keep the body alive, are diverted from the mouth and throat, making it difficult to talk or swallow. Blood flow is diverted away from the skin to the core of the body, supporting the internal organs and reducing blood loss if injured. This makes you cold and clammy, and the tightening of the skin causes your hair to stand on end. Digestion grinds to a halt, as an energy-saving measure. You have now been fully taken over by the stress response—ready to respond to danger. This brilliantly orchestrated symphony of bodily transformations has been honed by millions of years of natural selection. The stress response has only one job—to save your life in an immediate crisis—and it does it well. It will gear you up and usually get you out of trouble.

Nature has also developed a second response whose job it is to turn off all these intense reactions and return your body to normal after the tiger has slinked off seeking easier prey. This is called the *relaxation response*, and it resets the body to its pre-emergency state. It basically un-does all the work of the stress response, rendering you a plodding caveman or woman once again, happily crunching on a marrow-filled marmoset bone. Your worries are over—or, they would be, if it wasn't for the unhappy reality of something that may, in the long run, be almost as bad as a hungry tiger, and that is *chronic stress*.

Imaginary Dangers

Human beings evolved in a wide variety of environments, very few of which included telephones, traffic jams, 24-hour cable news channels, and international terrorists who tweet their jihad. While there were existential threats such as predators and starvation, the typical situation was one of, presumably, long periods of bucolic business-as-usual, punctuated by occasional terrors.[70] Acute stressors such as animal attacks are what the human nervous system (and that of most other animals as well) is built to deal with. In our current anthropogenic environment, however, we are subjected to *chronic stress*—a situation of unrelenting activation of the fight-or-flight mechanism—and that is an entirely different kettle of fish.

Being able to imagine the future (a faculty that scientists call *prospection*, as if we are imagining where to pan for gold) is one of the most defining features of primate 2.0, the human being.[71] We have the ability to construct scenarios in our head and act them out virtually. This has the very great advantage of meaning that we can choose in advance the course of action we think will be most desirable/successful. "How do I get across the river to hunt the buffalo? Hmmm…" The ability to plan has played a starring role in the human conquest of earth—it's been a big evolutionary success. So far.

However, like most upgrades, our planning ability comes with its own concomitant set of new problems. The important one here is that we can imagine future scenarios that are very troubling. You may be sitting at home in a warm, safe home, with a belly full of food, and absolutely no immediate problems, and yet you can be acutely distressed about the tax bill that you know will be coming nine months hence. Depending on your psychology, you can even be distressed about an impending alien invasion or the Rapture. In other words, our ability to imagine means that we can be worried about things that are not currently happening, and may never happen at all.

Although our stress response is essentially the same as that of almost all vertebrates, our cognitive capacities for imaging the future are unique. You will never see a fish worried about global warming. Your house cat can sleep blithely, ignorant of the probable outcome of the next election. Animals cannot imagine the future (beyond a few hours at most), and therefore are never stressed about it. If they have a problem, it's a literal, *physical threat in the current moment.* A human being can have a very stressful problem that's entirely *psychological* and located in an imaginary future. The threat may be real, in the sense that it can or will happen, but it is imaginary in the sense that it is not occurring in the present moment. Only the planning function allows us to imagine that it can or will happen.

Imaginary problems in a distant future are the cause of much chronic stress for human beings. We worry so much about the future that our stress response is on almost all of the time. And all of the advantages of the stress response—the beautiful things it does to our bodies in order to get us out of danger—become disadvantages when they continue over time. Chronic stress actually damages you both physically and psychologically. Chronic stimulation of the HPA system disrupts serotonin levels, and is a major factor in the development of depression and anxiety. The physical problems that can be caused or assisted by stress include heart disease, stroke, immune deficiency, cancer, serious gastrointestinal disorders, eating disorders, cancer, chronic pain, sexual and reproductive dysfunction, sleep disturbances, and other problems including allergies, skin problems, hair loss, periodontal disease, as well as increased probability of drug and alcohol addiction, and other unhealthy lifestyle choices. Clearly, chronic stress is a major cause of serious problems in our society, and drastically reduces our sense of wellbeing.

As perhaps the foremost expert on stress in the world, Robert Sapolsky of Stanford, puts it: "Indeed, when you look at the diseases that do us in, they are predominantly diseases that can be caused, or made worse, by stress. As a result, most of us... will have the profound Westernized luxury of dropping dead someday of a stress-related disease. That's why it's so urgent that we understand stress—and how to better manage it."[72]

Relaxation Meditation

The antidote to all this stress is already built into our systems: the relaxation response. Essentially the opposite of the stress response, the relaxation response breaks the cycle of chronic stress and brings you back to equilibrium. Many of us are so used to chronic stress that we might not even feel comfortable being relaxed at first. This paradox would be funny if it weren't so sad.

There are many ways to learn to manage stress, and begin reducing its negative effects on your body and brain. I won't insult your intelligence by listing all the effective ways to relax. It would be ridiculous to mention sleep, exercise, drink, vacation, nurturing good friendships, and other obvious and often-used methods. We'll only be looking at one particular technique of relaxation here, and that is meditation.

Meditation has long been associated with relaxation. In fact, many people think that relaxation is the main effect of meditation, when in fact there are many more. Almost any meditation technique can be relaxing. Mantra meditation, for example, can induce a strong relaxation response, mainly because it forces thoughts away from fantasizing about the future. Imaginary worry about future problems is one reason that so many spiritual teachers advise people to "stay in the present moment" or "be here now" so much. Activities that induce a concentrated state are relaxing for many reasons, one of which is that you are focused on something other than your imaginary problems.

The relaxation meditation you're going to learn next is relaxing for that reason, but it has a second, special further stress-reducing mechanism working in your favor. The technique is called Focus on

Relaxation. In the simplest description, you're relaxing your body and meditating on the bodily sensations of this relaxation.

Most of us enjoy relaxation, but we enter a kind of fuzzy, unclear state of semi-consciousness when the rest state becomes intense. That means that even though the relaxation is big, we're not enjoying it as much as we could. In this way of meditating, you're focusing your attention directly on the pleasant sensations of relaxation themselves. That is, you're attempting to become more aware of how they feel, not less aware. Becoming more aware of them tends to make these pleasant sensations even more pleasant, which induces more relaxation. And that gives you more to concentrate on and enjoy, etc. So at its best, this technique can induce a positive feedback loop which will make your relaxation go very deep—maybe deeper than you've ever consciously experienced. That's its special second mechanism. Focus on Relaxation is a basic, but nevertheless powerful, technique that will do a lot to begin manifesting the benefits of life-improvement for you.

Don't expect that you will feel like you've just had two weeks of sleeping in late, getting massages, sitting in a hot tub, and drinking margaritas on your first try. Even though the very deep relaxation I described is a real possibility, it can take some time to manifest. So don't make the depth of your relaxation a big deal at first. Even if you become just a little less tense—even one percent less tense— while doing the following meditation technique, that counts as relaxation. If you're relaxing even a tiny bit, then you are doing the technique correctly.

In the long run, this may be the only meditation technique you ever need. Why? Because if you're like most Americans, you are suffering from overwork, a chronic lack of sleep, and a tremendous amount of stress. Focus on Relaxation will help with all three of these challenges. While you're doing it, you're not working, and it will strongly relieve stress. It will even give you a few of the benefits of sleep, because you are resting deeply. I would recommend that if you are chronically under-rested, you get some sleep instead of meditating. Under those conditions, probably nothing will improve your life more than simply getting adequate shut-eye every day. Once you are rested, however, this meditation can work wonders to reduce your stress, help you feel calm, and get the most out of life. Let's look at how to actually do that now.

Ready for some relaxation? The essence of this technique is to relax your muscles and to meditate on the sensations of them relaxing. That's it. You may well wonder how this meditation differs from a progressive relaxation exercise, or a nap for that matter. It's different in a significant way—you are making the experience of relaxation *conscious*. During a nap, you are very relaxed, but you are unconscious (i.e. asleep) the whole time.

A progressive relaxation exercise is much closer to what you are doing here, but there are differences. For one, you are putting more effort into focusing on the relaxation and getting a lot of clarity about how it feels in your body. Secondly, it's fine to fall asleep in a progressive relaxation, and here you're attempting to stay awake.

By making these unconscious processes conscious, you'll enjoy them more deeply and get better at inducing them at will. You will also be developing your three elements of concentration, sensory clarity, and acceptance, so it will increase your skill at every other sort of meditation as well. This all makes the Focus on Relaxation technique a uniquely powerful way to work.

Before you sit, remember to turn off your phone, any messaging, and all other distractions. Preferably do this in a quiet room in which you will not be disturbed. You want to be able to relax in a safe and comfortable environment.

FOCUS ON RELAXATION — GUIDED TECHNIQUE

Before you begin, find your meditation seat, either sitting in a chair, on a bench, a cushion, or the floor.

Sit up straight, extending your spine upwards toward the ceiling. Make sure your chin is pointing just slightly (5 degrees) below horizontal.

Next relax your entire body. Take three deep breaths, and let each one of them out long and slowly.

Now you're ready to begin the Focus on Relaxation practice. Relax your scalp and forehead. Feel the actual muscles in this region releasing. Do the meditation algorithm on this area for several rounds. The focus object is the body sensation of the muscles themselves letting go.

For each of the areas mentioned next, do the same thing as above.

Next relax the muscles all around your eyes.

Now your cheeks and jaw muscles.

Relax your throat and voice box.

Release your neck and shoulders, and let them settle into a relaxed position.

Next, let go of any sense that you're going to do anything with your arms and hands. Instead, allow them to come into a gentle, open, repose. Starting with the right arm, relax your upper arm, then your forearm, then your hand, then your fingers. Give each of these regions several rounds of the meditation algorithm before moving on. Then do the same thing with your left arm and hand.

Now relax the muscles of your upper chest. This includes the front of the chest, the sides, and the upper back. Relax this entire region to the best of your ability.

Now relax all of the muscles of your middle abdomen. This includes the belly region, the sides of the body (above the waist), and the kidney area of the back. Relax this entire region to the best of your ability.

Next release all of the tension in your pelvic region. Focus especially on the large muscles of the hip joints. These big muscles will feel very good when they relax.

Next, let go of any sense that you're going to do anything with your legs and feet. Instead, allow them to come into a gentle, open repose. Starting with the right leg, relax your thigh, then your calf, then your foot, then your toes. Give each of these regions several rounds of the meditation algorithm before moving on. Then do the same thing with your left leg and foot.

Now, feel relaxation in the entire body at once. Connect with the sensations of being relaxed, open, loose, supple, soft, gentle, and released in all of the muscles of your body.
Continue with this for as long as you like.

When it's time to finish, spend at least one minute just sitting quietly, meditating on relaxed sensations in the body before continuing on with your day.

CHAPTER ELEVEN

Beyond High Hopes

In order to get the benefits of meditation, you have to actually do it. That's why it's called a practice. All the theory and reading in the world won't give you what you're looking for, but a few minutes of sitting and doing the practice each day actually will.

As an integral part of reading this book, I suggest that you do at least 10 minutes of meditation each day. There are guided 10-minute audio versions of all the meditations in the book on my website. There are also 30-minute versions in case you want to sit longer. Please make use of these in order to help yourself establish a regular sitting practice.

When I first learned to meditate, I was so full of high hopes, excitement, and the thrill of a challenge, I meditated often. In high school, I had run the 440 yard race and anchored the Mile Relay. Training for those races was challenging, and it felt good sometimes. Running in all those track meets had been fun. Sometimes our relay team did well, and that was a blast.

Meditation training reminds me of training for a track race. The important difference with meditation is that there's never a race. It's not really training for any specific event in the future. Instead, it's training for *every* event in the future. It's upgrading your abilities to succeed at whatever activities you do all day, every day, for the rest of your life.

That's a real benefit, but it also has a strange downside. Even though my new meditation practice was really improving my wellbeing, over time, it started to lose priority as a practice. I started sort of taking it for granted. Friends wanted to do things, and I would make time by skipping meditation "just this once." A girlfriend wanted to go away for a weekend, and meditation would be forgotten for two or three days. Because there was no specific event that I was training for, I found it hard to keep the importance of daily meditation clear in my mind.

The trouble is that you have to practice meditation almost every day—at least five days a week—to fully reap the benefits of the mindfulness we've been discussing. Meditation is much more like brushing your teeth or taking a shower than training for a marathon. The best mindset is to just make it an integral part of your daily routine.

Establishing and maintaining that kind of steady, daily practice presents a challenge, even for people with a strong motivation to sit. Understanding some basic psychological principles, however, can help you to create and maintain the regular practice you desire. A few simple brain hacks can nudge your meditation tendency over the line to a sustainable, lifelong practice. Here are seven methods that do just that:

Make a Contract with Yourself — There's this funny thing about the brain. It really dislikes things that make it look contradictory or hypocritical. This naturally applies socially, but it turns out that you want to appear consistent even to yourself. This is related to a psychological principle called "consistency theory" and here's how to make it work in your favor.[73]

Write up a contract with yourself, explicitly committing to meditate every day. Then sign it. Put this contract in a place where you can see it. You will actually begin to change your beliefs and actions to come into line with this written commitment. Even when you don't feel like meditating—there's a concert, or a date, or sleeping late, or whatever you would rather do—somewhere in the back of your mind you will remember that contract, and that can push you over the edge toward sitting down and meditating first before you go. Of course, you must be serious about honoring your contract, and being honest with yourself.

Make a Calendar — You can make your written commitment even stronger if you create a calendar each week, containing specific meditation goals for each day. Draw a checkbox each day, and label it with something like "15 minutes of meditation." Post this calendar prominently, in a place where you see it all the time, and put a large X in the box after you sit. It can be satisfying to put that X in the box, and it feels good to look back on a week of completed sits. Combining this calendar with the contract makes both work more effectively. A lightweight alternative for a calendar could be as simple as a meditation item included on your daily task list.

There are also several excellent applications that not only serve as a meditation calendar, but that remind you to do it. On Windows, Outlook or Lightning can be used to create a meditation calendar, and are integrated with email clients you may already have. If you want a stand-alone Windows program that's also free, Rainlender[74] comes highly recommended. (I haven't used any of these programs myself). On my Mac, I really like the Todo program from Appigio.[75] Cross-platform, by far the best web-based application is Google Calendar. All of these can send you reminders to motivate you to sit down and meditate.

There are also, of course, many dedicated smartphone apps that have this functionality as well.[76] Because most of these include some "gamification" (point scoring, achievement ranks, special challenges, badges, etc.) aspects. they may be even more effective as motivators.

Social Pressure — You've made a contract and signed it, and you've got a meditation calendar up and running. You may be using a smartphone app. With these tools helping you to stay motivated and engaged in your meditation practice, the next step is to publicly state your dedication to meditation. Never underestimate the power of social or peer pressure. It magnifies the effect of consistency theory because we especially want to appear consistent to others. When you commit in public to doing something, you will make bigger efforts to do what you said you would.

There are many ways to do this. Post on Facebook and Twitter. Tell your friends and family. Make a commitment in front of your twelve-step group. Repeatedly tell your therapist. Find someone with similar aspirations and become "accountability buddies" for each other. Obviously, do this without annoying people, making it seem like you're better than them somehow, or being arrogant. The idea is simply to state your intention, for example, to sit every day for the next 90 days. Then give updates maybe once a month on how you're doing. This works so well, that the hardest part is simply continuing once the 90 days is over. Feel free to then start anew by making a yearlong commitment.

Sit with a Group — If you want to get the full benefit of social pressure, join a meditation group. On top of the gain you get from consistency theory, you will also benefit from a major increase in your desire to meditate, due to the normative effects of peer pressure. I always say that "half of who you are is other people," meaning that the beliefs, attitudes, and biases of the people around you gradually become your own. By intentionally surrounding yourself with people who meditate, who believe that meditation is a good thing to do, who talk about the details of practice, and so forth, you are slowly and subtly reprogramming yourself to be a long term meditator.

And there's the benefit of the group's meditation schedule, which also helps to keep you on track. There are plenty of mindfulness meditation groups who practice something similar to what is described in this book.[77] Most of these will have a Buddhist religious orientation, however, so prepare for that. (I offer meditation classes for those who want to practice with a non-religious group of mindful geeks. You can find those at themindfulgeek.net.) Meditating in a group has the added benefit of giving you an opportunity to discuss your practice with others, which can be helpful.

Make It Hard to Fail — Sometimes it's really hard to keep practicing. For example, in the past, I've traveled to India for meditation intensives. These trips were expensive—both in time and money— and required engineering my entire life around making such excursions possible. I was extremely dedicated, and willing to make almost any sacrifice. Long flights, uncomfortable travel, and intense dysentery—I experienced it all with almost a sense of joy, because I felt that it was part of my meditation journey, and therefore, meaningful to me.

One time, however, after overcoming seemingly insurmountable obstacles, I finally arrived at a temple in rural Gujarat. It was located in a very remote and impoverished village. I had practiced there before and felt that I had a pretty good understanding of what to expect. It would be dirty and uncomfortable, the food would either be unpalatable or almost non-existent, it would be impossible to sleep. There would be scorpions, bees, hundred-degree heat, interruptions, no hot water, and sometimes no water at all. All of this I was ready for, figuring it was all worth it. I had come to love this village and its people, and figured that I would have a month of intensive meditation in blissful silence.

But this time, there was a new challenge awaiting me. The temple had recently purchased a new sound system. This in a village where most homes were constructed of rough wood and mud with floors of smoothed cow dung, and almost no house had electricity or running water. Because they had gotten hooked up to the electricity grid, the temple rigged a microphone and ran in through a soundboard to some speakers. These speakers were like something you might find on a battleship at sea: large cones that only captured the most penetrating treble notes. It was the most blaring, ugly, ear-shattering sound system imaginable.

After all the money, the travel, the difficulties, I had just settled into my meditation spot, and was getting ready for a solid month of practice. With growing unease, I heard the sound system getting put into place, but was relieved that it was only an hour or two a day of them experimenting with it. I meditated as best I could during the other hours, and weathered the storm the rest of the time. I figured it would be tough, but I could still get my "money's worth" out of the retreat.

But the next day, it all fell apart. The head priest of the temple somehow acquired an electronic keyboard; a Casiotone. The smallest, cheapest, and most hideous-sounding keyboard. This he played next to the microphone, broadcasting its squeaks and squawks through the monstrous sound system and out into the dusty Indian day. He didn't know any songs, he simply noodled around on the instrument, without tempo, tonality, or intention. And he proceeded to do it, more or less, continuously for days. He must have been letting other people take over at various times. It seemed as though the whole village was agog over the sound system and the miraculous Casiotone, because they never stopped. On one level it was kind of hilarious and awesome.

Sequestered away in my meditation cell, however, each bleat from the keyboard was like a stab of pain in my guts. I just kept thinking of the wasted hours of my retreat, all of the wasted money and effort getting to India, the trek all the way out to this remote region to practice. All for nothing. I was devastated. It seemed that there was no way out of spending my entire retreat listening to an atonal cacophonous concert at ear-splitting volume. Giving diplomacy a try, I spoke to the head priest, who was surrounded by friends and admirers, all of whom were focused on the music. Would it be possible, I asked, to play a little less music? They smiled and pointed at the keyboard and the sound system. Wasn't it wonderful? Wasn't it just the greatest thing? The head priest, who I liked a lot, just smiled and played more for me. I got the point that it wasn't going to stop anytime soon, and slunk back to my room.

Having nothing else to do, and having made a commitment to practice, however, I just kept sitting there. I did my best to meditate, hour after hour, day after day. Slowly, something began to happen. I began to get tired of hating and resisting the music. It was just too hard to stay upset about it. And I noticed that the less I resisted it, the less it bothered me. It was still a terrible racket, like a hundred calliopes falling down a staircase, amplified through something you might find at a stadium rock concert. But slowly, it didn't bother me as much, and eventually, it didn't bother me at all. I was able to get as much, if not more, from that retreat than with any other.

The moral of this story is the importance of cultivating acceptance in meditation practice. But there is another lesson, which is that it would have been very easy for me to have given up and gone home. Often, the reasons that make it challenging to maintain a consistent meditation practice are quite mundane: your cat won't leave you alone, your neighbor plays loud music, the phone keeps ringing. In day-to-day meditating, these little things can grow big enough to frustrate even the most dedicated person. It's important to minimize all such annoyances by intelligently engineering your practice times and places. Sit at the quietest times of day, unplug the phone and the computer, let your partner know that you don't want to be disturbed, put the cat outside. Don't make it necessary for you to go to extremes to get your practice done; instead do everything possible to make it easy to keep going. By reducing the number of reasons to stop sitting, you'll be increasing your likelihood of success with meditation.

Work with a Meditation Coach — Sure, you can teach yourself to play the guitar or master your golf game. But complex, nuanced tasks like these are much easier to learn with the help of a qualified coach, and meditation is no exception. An experienced meditation teacher can help you with your practice in a number of important ways— avoiding pitfalls, sensitizing you to growth areas, keeping you from deluding yourself about problem areas—but one of the most useful is helping you stay committed to a regular practice. Knowing that you're going to have to check in and report on your progress to another person is a very strong incentive to sit down and meditate.

Once a Week, Consciously List the Goals and Benefits of Mediation Practice — Sometimes you will be having trouble getting motivated to sit down and meditate, and the question will suddenly pop into your head, "Why am I even doing this stupid practice in the first place?" And often you won't be able to find the answer to this question at hand. Your mind just draws a blank on the topic. Then your commitment to your practice begins unraveling.

I recommend journaling about why you're meditating (the reasons may change over time) and what concrete benefits you've gotten from meditation recently. Do this weekly if you can, or at least once a month. For one thing, you will notice that you are getting a lot more benefit from your practice than you may have realized. For another, you will have a motivating answer ready at the crucial moment when you ask yourself why you're even doing it.

You're meditating to improve your life, and to experience a greater sense of wellbeing. If you remember that, then all this effort to reinforce daily practice will make good sense and keep you on track. You will move beyond high hopes, into the reality of daily achievement in your meditation practice. All it takes is committing to between 10 and 30 minutes of practice at least five times a week. When you find that you are really making that happen over time, and you are getting the benefits of your efforts, it will feel excellent.

CHAPTER TWELVE

Take Your Body with You

In the Bay Area, where I live, there are a lot of dance events. The DJs are incredible, the music is made for movement, and the scene is friendly and fun. It allows me to let go and move my body in the ways that it feels like moving—not in some set of rote dance steps, but instead just feeling what I'm feeling and letting that express outwardly as movement. It's a very direct, simple, natural way to experience the body.

Yet this simple way of relating to your body has been all but lost for most adults. How often do you move your body at all, except to fulfill some task? Even in sports, most of the motions are pre-programmed, to the point where training for sports becomes training your body to move only in a certain, optimized way. I love yoga, but sometimes think about how rigid and defined each pose is. There's very little freedom of movement in our culture. And, worse yet, many people barely move at all. For many people, a typical day means sitting in a car, sitting at work, and sitting on the couch. We don't pay too much attention to our bodies, but meditation on the body can help us reclaim our embodied awareness.

Paying attention to the body is a radical act. We tend to think of the mind as transcendent, clean, pure, and perfect, whereas the body is limited, unclean, impure, and imperfect. Like it or not, the Judeo-Christian religious forms that underlie our culture see the body as a sinful, even Satanic object, as opposed to the holy, disembodied soul. Our society seems designed to point your attention away from the body and toward the mind. We reward the people who are the most mental.

Yet in mindfulness meditation, paying attention to the body is incredibly important. When you first begin to tune into body sensations in meditation, your mind will probably resist. Rather than feeling the body directly, it will usually try to *think about* the body. It will create mental pictures of the body parts and then imagine that they should be different. It may also get involved in a lot of imagination about medical conditions or illness. That's what the mind does: it worries about the body, dislikes it, or tries to change it.

When I first started meditating in 1980, I had a very hard time sitting still. Upon attempting to actually sit, however, I was shocked to discover that my dreams of ecstasy did not immediately manifest. I fidgeted. I itched. It was boring. I coughed. My hips hurt. My mind wandered. My legs fell asleep. I fidgeted some more. The sad reality was that sitting still was uncomfortable and even hurt.

This made me mad at my body. Here I was trying to transcend my petty ego and its desires, and the weakness of my body was holding me back. I persisted with my meditating, and as the years progressed, I developed a kind of adversarial relationship with my body. Many aspects of the traditional meditative literature and culture help to do this. My job as a meditator was (supposedly) to exert my will over the body, with its sad, earthly weaknesses and needs, and to force it to sit still while I worked on purifying my mind. In short: my body was the problem.

It took me a long time and a lot of meditation to discover that the body is not the problem. In fact, the body is a vital part of the solution. Mindfulness is not a matter of the transcendental mind overcoming the earthly body. It involves becoming reacquainted, familiar, and kind to the body. This is a bit harder than it sounds, but by understanding it from the very beginning, you can save yourself years of hardship and struggle. With a little guidance, even the first steps can be relatively easy. And when you begin to really touch the body deeply, to connect with it, to know it inside out, to accept it, even to love it, you will begin to be at home in your skin, and at home in the world.

In my experience, many of us geeky types have a harder time than others contacting the body directly. It may be that mentally-focused, logic-prone people discover early that they're better at conceptual tasks than physical ones, and shift their attention away from the body. How many nerds can relate to getting praise their whole lives for being smart, and experiencing shame around sports and other body-centric activities? Whatever its genesis, contacting the body is a particular challenge for non-kinesthetic people, but one that therefore has a greater payoff once it's accomplished. So let's look at what contacting the body entails.

If I told you that meditating on something was different than thinking about it, you'd probably say, Duh, you already knew that. Yet when people first meditate on the body, that's often exactly what they do: they think about it. We are so at home in our thinking that we've almost lost the ability to contact bodily sensation. When people meditate on the physical body, they might feel some body sensation, but they'll also tend to experience a lot of mental images of the body. Pictures of the positions of their limbs, mental images of the shape of their torso, and so on. And these mental images are thoughts, not physical sensations.

Meditating on the body means meditating on body sensation, not on mental images of the body. If you close your eyes and meditate on the bottoms of your feet right now, notice that you can feel the bottoms of your feet, but you may also be experiencing a mental picture of your feet. That mental image of your feet is fine and natural, but in meditating on the body, it's important to not focus on that. Don't push it away, don't get angry at it, but simply don't focus on that. Instead, allow your attention to focus on the *feeling* of the bottoms of your feet. The actual physical sensations. Concentrate on just that sensation, letting go of noticing mental images.

I was recently in Zürich, Switzerland, and visited a famous landmark called Grossmünster Cathedral. Outside in the square, I found an unusual object: a three-foot long bronze model of the cathedral, mounted on a plinth. Why have a model of the cathedral when the cathedral is right there? But then I spotted a brass plaque with writing in both letters and in Braille. It said that the model was for blind people to "visit" the cathedral with their hands; to feel its shape, its contours, its uniqueness.

This is exactly the way to encounter body sensation: like a person who's been blind from birth. You reach out with body sensation and feel the interior and exterior contours of the body, like a blind person exploring a cathedral model. You get into the actual, earthly contact of body sensation; you feel it in the meat, so to speak. Not in your head, not in your imagination. In your body. You try to feel all the little details.

Notice if you can feel the sensation in the bottoms of your feet in that way. There are the pads of the toes, the soles, the arches, and the solidity of the heels. Feel each area of sensation individually. And then feel them together again. This is actual contact with body sensation. This is meditating on the body. This is where to begin.

When you meditate on the body in this way, it is vital that you learn to listen to the body as the body. You listen to it speaking in its native tongue, so to speak. What is the native language of the body? Its machine code? The native language of the body is *sensation*. It is feeling. If you want to deeply understand a foreign culture, the only way to do it is to learn the language. It's the same with the body. If you really want to become mindful of body sensations, you have to learn to understand the language of the body. And what the body says in its native language may be very different from the things the mind says about it.

For example, we all have a mental image of the size of our various body parts, and a mental image about the size of the body in general. Yet often in mindfulness meditation, the body or parts of the body can feel larger or smaller than the mind knows them to be. You might feel that your body sensation extends outside the known limits of your skin. It can feel sometimes as if you are much taller than you actually are, or as if your body is expanding outward like a balloon, inches or yards beyond your actual outline. If this happens, don't try to correct that feeling or (on the other hand) to imagine that it means something cosmic. It just means that you're tuning into the "felt sensation" of the body, which is different than the mental picture of the body.

Another unusual way the body talks about itself is that it doesn't always feel like it's a standard human body. Sometimes it can feel like your legs turn into a ball or your entire body becomes a big, beanbag-like object. Again, this doesn't mean anything special, and yet it's not a mistake, either. It's just the body feeling the way it does at the moment. No big.

A third way that the body may surprise you is that it can feel like it's changing, morphing, or moving. For example, your hand might feel like it is tingling, or like waves are moving through it, or like it's growing and shrinking. These can be very unusual sensations at first, and yet the more that you sit with the body, the more you realize that they are part of its native language. It's very easy to get all trippy about what these changing sensations mean (whole schools of meditation focus their supposed significance), but to me they are simply the body feeling the way it does. Sometimes it just feels like it's rippling, bubbling, wavy, moving, tingling, growing/shrinking, or other things your mind knows it's not actually doing. It's no big deal. To make them mean more than that is the mind trying to impose its ideas on the body again.

Meditating on the body, then, is a bit like dancing. It's not about feeling a certain way, or getting the body to do what you want it to.

It's about feeling how you feel, and not judging it, "correcting" it, or trying to change it. Instead, just accept the fact that your thoughts about the body and its characteristics and how it should be are sometimes very different than the actual feelings that occur in the body. Recognizing these differences is important; it's part of the self-knowledge and understanding aspect of meditation. Your job is not to cover up or resolve these differences, but instead to accept and validate both viewpoints. It's a kind of acceptance—one of the key elements of meditation. It's not possible to simultaneously experience the body as it is and to be dedicated to rejecting and changing how it is. You have to open up to letting body sensations express whatever and however they want to. That's the only way to ever sink more deeply into the actual experience of body sensation.

Focus on Body Sensation Meditation

I've made the point of how important it is to tune into body sensations. It's important that you try to let go of resistance to body sensations. Just accept them however they are. Give them all the room in the world to be whatever they want to be. The idea is to maintain an attitude of curiosity toward body sensations. Good or bad, pleasant or unpleasant, open up to exploring them however they are manifesting right now.

A major part of this exploration is to work on sensory clarity. To do this, you attempt to explore each sensation in as much detail as possible. First, notice where the sensation feels like it's located. Notice that I used the word "feels" here. That means it's not a mental picture of where it's located, but a sensation in the body of where it's located.

Next notice the felt size of the sensation. Does it feel like it's the size of a baseball? A grain of sand? A basketball?

What is its shape? Does it feel spherical, cubic, or like it's some more complex shape? Remember that bodies are three dimensional, and body sensations are therefore also three-dimensional. You may be able to tease apart the difference between the surface of the sensation and the inside of the sensation. Different places within the sensation may feel different. For example the upper left may feel tighter, say, than the lower right. Or the center may feel "goopy" while the outer layers feel "crunchy." And so on.

Feel the texture of the sensation. Is it hard or soft? Smooth or bumpy or wavy? Goopy or crusty? In what ways do different areas of the sensation feel different from each other?

These are just some suggestions of ways to get curious about the qualities of a body sensation. By exploring a sensation in this way, you will over time greatly increase your sensory clarity. Let's try meditating on the body now.

FOCUS ON BODY SENSATION — GUIDED TECHNIQUE

Before you begin, find your meditation seat, either sitting in a chair, on a bench, a cushion, or the floor.

Sit up straight, extending your spine upwards toward the ceiling. Make sure your chin is pointing just slightly (5 degrees) below horizontal.

Next relax your entire body. Take three deep breaths, and let each one of them out long and slowly.

Now you're ready to begin the Focus on Body Sensation practice.

Start by feeling the sensations in your scalp and forehead. Tune into the sensations in the skin, the muscles, the bone in this region. Do the meditation algorithm on this area for several rounds. For each of the areas mentioned below, do the same thing as above.

Next feel the body sensations all around your eyes.

Now your cheeks and jaw muscles.

Feel the sensations in your throat and voice box.

Feel the body sensations in your neck and shoulders. Accept whatever you find there.

Next, let go of any sense that you're going to do anything with your arms and hands. Instead, allow them to come into a gentle, open, repose. Starting with the right arm, feel the body sensations in your upper arm, then your forearm, then your hand, then your fingers.

Give each of these regions several rounds of the meditation algorithm before moving on. Then do the same thing with your left arm and hand.

Now feel the sensations in the muscles of your upper chest. This includes the front of the chest, the sides (near the armpits), and the upper back. Feel into this entire region to the best of your ability.

Now feel the body sensations in all the muscle of your middle abdomen. This includes the belly region, the sides of the body (above the waist), and the kidney area of the back. Allow awareness to contact this entire region to the best of your ability.

Next feel the body sensations in your pelvic region. Focus especially on the large muscles of the hip joints. Remember that body sensations are three-dimensional, and you may be able to contact sensations both inside and on the surface of these big muscles.

Next, let go of any sense that you're going to do anything with your legs and feet. Instead, allow them to come into a gentle, open, repose. Starting with the right leg, feel the sensations in your thigh, then your calf, then your foot, then your toes. Give each of these regions several rounds of the meditation algorithm before moving on. Then do the same thing with your left leg and foot.

Now, zoom out with your awareness, and feel the sensations in the entire body at once. Accept whatever sensations you find there. Allow them to be exactly how they are. Do not try to change or resist them.

Continue with this for as long as you like.

When it's time to finish, spend at least one minute just sitting quietly, meditating on sensations in the body before continuing on with your day.

VARIATION: BREATH MEDITATION

Many traditions use focus on the breath as their main meditation technique. When you think about it, body sensations of breathing are simply a subset of all body sensation. If you want to meditate on breath sensations, do it exactly like the meditation above, but restricting your attention to just the body sensations associated with breathing.

CHAPTER THIRTEEN

Meditation in Life

If you lift weights at the gym, over time, your muscles will become a lot stronger. But imagine if, when you left the gym at the end of a workout, your muscles shrunk back to their previous size so that you couldn't use that extra strength in regular life. Some people might find the workout intrinsically fun or pleasant, but I think most people would soon give up on it. Why spend the effort to lift weights if you don't get the benefits of stronger muscles all day long? Luckily, when you build a muscle at the gym, it stays strong during all the other activities of your life. It's not just good for weight lifting, it's also good for, say, lifting heavy boxes, playing sports, and looking attractive. It's generally useful.

The same thing is true with meditation. Many people find meditation intrinsically pleasant, and would probably do it for its own sake. But the skills you cultivate in meditation are not just restricted to being useful during a formal sit. The concentration abilities you gain continue to function when you're at work or play, helping you to focus better on whatever you're interested in. Sensory clarity is a huge boon whenever you're interacting with other people, because it helps you to understand what they're feeling and thereby connect with them more deeply. It's also great for enjoying the finer things in life: it is the ability which really lets you dig into the tastes of dinner, the beauty of art, the sound of music, the feeling of making love. Sensory clarity engenders a richer, more fulfilling, more meaningful life. And the quality of acceptance that you build during meditation is, perhaps, the most useful skill of all. Being able to let go and accept things for what they are is the essence of fun, of play, of engagement in life. It's the opposite of the OCD, always dissatisfied, high-anxiety lifestyle of most of us.

Life often asks us to wait, and a lot of this waiting can feel crushingly pointless. We cool our heels in lines at the supermarket, the bank, or at a restaurant. We spend hours stuck in traffic, held up in airports, or sitting at a desk. I find wasted time to be an unpleasant experience. Life is too short to be eaten up by all these dull, meaningless moments. These days we have the option of zoning out into our smartphones, but I contend that playing *Candy Crush Soda* while lingering in the doctor's office doesn't really give much meaning to that half an hour. It's still a waste of precious time, albeit a pleasant one.

A much more powerful way to engage these moments is to practice on your meditation skills as you go about your day. With a little bit of adaptability, you can gain valuable and effective meditation practice while watching the clock hands crawl at the DMV. Do simple (and safe) meditation exercises while you're stuck in traffic or waiting at the airport. Every formerly wasted moment can become a part of your mindfulness training regimen. Here are some possibilities:

Breathe — This standard-issue meditation practice has a lot going for it, including the fact that you can do it almost continuously while going about your business. Just tune into the body sensations associated with the act of breathing, while continuing to breathe normally. Feel the raising and lowering of your rib cage, the movement of the diaphragm, the rush of air in your nostrils, and so forth. You'll notice how your breath quickens in certain situations, but actually seizes up in others—remember to just keep breathing.

Feel Your Emotions — Meditating on emotional body sensations is a little more challenging, but has several advantages that make it worth the effort. You contact the place in your body where it feels like an emotion is happening. For example, if you are happy, you might feel your face lighting up in a smile, or an uplifting feeling in your chest. Continuous contact with emotions in the body keeps you aware of how you're feeling moment by moment—something that many of us could use more of. This technique also allows you to notice when unpleasant emotions die down or fade away entirely—often accompanied by a soft wave of relaxation and relief.

Listen — Most people imagine that mindfulness means only focusing inwardly, but you can just as easily focus on external sensory events. For example, it's relaxing and stimulating to open your ears and listen to the sounds around you without judgment. The trick here is to not focus on any particular sound, but to hear everything together at once. It's a sound bath that is ever changing and ever fresh.

Driving — This is another externally focused practice that you can do while in the car. It combines the listening practice above with intentional seeing. Not only do you listen to what's going on around you, you also concentrate on the visual activity of driving. You pay close attention to the relevant details of the road, the signage, the movement of the other cars around you, and so forth. Especially if you are a commuter, this can add hours of valuable meditation practice to your day. It's very important, however, to remember to only meditate on things that help you drive your car effectively. *Extra credit* if you can focus on any body sensations relevant to driving also. These would include such things as the feeling of your feet on the pedals, the sensations of acceleration and deceleration, the feeling of your hands on the steering wheel, and so on.

These meditation-in-motion practices will seriously up the hours per week you spend doing something useful and positive. They may even help you to be more present in every situation and experience of your life. And that's the goal.

CHAPTER FOURTEEN

Acceptance

When I was in India, we often sat flat on the floor instead of on a meditation cushion. After maybe a half an hour of that, my knees would start complaining. After several hours, they were screaming. Meditating on anything besides pain was very difficult. At the end of the day, I would practically hobble to my room, bathed in relief to finally be done. But then next morning, my knees hurt the moment I sat down. And that would begin another long day meditating on physical pain. Not only did this teach me a lot about working with pain, but also a lot about acceptance.

When you're meditating, difficult experiences may sometimes come up. You might feel some physical pain. You might have some unpleasant emotions or negative thoughts. Meditation pries the lid off of your unconscious mind, which is a good thing. It allows you to understand yourself very deeply. It can be a catalyst for healing a lot of psychological difficulties, and is crucial to improving your wellbeing. But the unconscious is also the place you hide away all the difficult material that you don't want to deal with. So coming into contact with that hidden stuff, or even just the normal, everyday stuff, can be unpleasant at times.

In mindfulness meditation, you try to accept every experience. Even if the experience is unpleasant, negative, or unsettling, you attempt to accept it as it is. That's why the meditation algorithm includes the acceptance step—it reminds you often to let go of any resistance to whatever you're meditating upon.

Acceptance is the key to real growth in meditation. All of the practices in this book are effective to some degree at improving your life. Different people respond better to some than to others, but they all work well. If, however, I had to choose just one thing out of this whole book, a single practice to give someone to most improve their life, it would be the practice of acceptance. In my opinion, acceptance has the most power to positively impact your sense of wellbeing. You can practice acceptance as part of meditation and also as you walk around in daily life.

To demonstrate what I mean by acceptance, do a little experiment with me. Close your fists as tightly as you can. Squeeze them hard until it almost hurts. Furrow your brow and scowl. Say, forcefully, the word, "NO" several times. Really mean it.

Now open your hands. Just let them relax. Let your face relax, too, except perhaps for the trace of a smile. Gently say the word, "Yes," several times. Really mean it. Open up and say, "Yes."

Feel the difference between these two states? The first is resistance, the second is allowing. Acceptance, for all it's talked about, is really that simple. It's as easy as opening your hands, relaxing, and saying, "Yes." It's letting go of resistance. Yet acceptance is also the practice that students tend to resist most. People just don't like the idea of accepting things. To "passively submit" to anything seems to go against the grain of our society. We admire people who fight hard against cancer, even when they are bound to die. We make heroes out of people who refuse to accept the adverse conditions of their lives, and who strive against all odds to change those conditions for the better. This kind of struggle to improve the world and our place in it is beautiful and laudable, and worth all of the blood, sweat, and tears shed in achieving it. By all means, work hard to change your life and the world for the better. Even the goal of this book is to change your life for the better, so clearly I think that this sort of effort is a good thing.

If we are going to have a rational discourse on this topic, however, we have to admit that there are, in fact, some things that we cannot change. If it is raining, and you don't want it to rain, there is not much you can do about it. Changing the weather just isn't an option.

And yet, I sometimes run into people who are actively angry about the weather. They want it to be hotter or colder, they want it to snow or to stop snowing, they want it to be less or more windy. And they're entitled to their emotions about it. Yet, in the case of things we cannot change, wouldn't it be better if we could generate a little acceptance of the situation? All the anger, sorrow, and other negative emotions about the weather are never going to change anything, it's only going to make you unhappy. In such a situation, acceptance is not only reasonable, but a very desirable strategy.

There are much more serious things which are just as unchangeable as the weather. Injury, aging, death. No matter how hard you struggle, you're not going to be able to fight your way out of these difficult realities. We know with 100 percent certainty that you will at some point get injured, at some point get old, and at some point cease to be (barring any immortality breakthroughs in our near future). It's just part of life. Yet the Dylan Thomas lines *"Do not go gentle into that good night / …/ rage, rage against the dying of the light!"* perfectly expresses our cultural position on death. Fight it tooth and nail to the finish.

What about things that aren't as clear-cut as aging and death? What about situations that it seems we have some small measure control over, but which still aren't turning out as we might fervently wish them to? I knew a man who had struggled for years to help his stepdaughter, who was a junkie, overcome her addiction. He had spent money for multiple rehabs, for lawyers, for therapy. He had been there for her emotionally in all those situations and more. He had gotten her new jobs after she'd lost others, new homes after she'd been kicked out of others. He had done everything a loving parent could think of doing. And the end result was that she ended up years later still addicted, but also hating him and refusing to speak to him. What more could he do in a situation like that? There is only so much recrimination and self-doubt and wishing for things to be different that a person can engage in. Eventually, even if you are going to continue to work for a positive outcome, you simply have to accept the situation as it is for the moment.

Then there are things like slavery, economic disparity, racial and sexual discrimination, the destruction of the environment, and other tragic circumstances. Unlike, say, death, there is something we can do about these conditions, and would be remiss if we didn't fight to change these things with every effort we can muster. At the same time, it is really necessary or helpful to feel personally upset about these conditions every moment of the day? Living in the Bay Area, I know a lot of activists, and some of them are almost never happy. Instead they're angry, upset, and sad about the state of the world virtually every waking hour. It seems like there must be some kind of middle ground, where it's possible to accept that horrible conditions are the way they are right at this moment, and also to work diligently to change them in the future.

Accepting all of these unpleasant things doesn't have to feel like giving up or losing in some way. They are part of the way life is. Accepting death is like accepting gravity. It's just built into the universe. Fighting it is absurd, counterproductive, and will not improve your wellbeing. Accepting these things, on the other hand, will go a long way toward making you feel better each day. Accept them in the spirit of acknowledging reality; the spirit of seeing things as they really are.

You may have found the previous few paragraphs unsettling. Most of us are in such a state of resistance and non-acceptance about these simple-but-awful facts that we push them down into the unconscious. We live in a state of denial about them. On some level, we feel that if we just live right—if we just make enough money, if we just do X, Y, and Z—then nothing bad will happen to us or the people we love. This attitude means that the facts of the situation have been submerged beneath the surface of awareness, into the deep waters of the unconscious. That's where meditation comes in.

Resistance

In the context of meditation practice, you can think of two kinds of acceptance. Acceptance One is experienced in the body as some degree of physical relaxation. Your body is not tensing against an experience, whether physical or mental. Acceptance Two is experienced in the mind, as a lack of psychological resistance. Psychological resistance could take the form of certain types of mental talk ("This sucks. This shouldn't be happening. I've got to get out of here.") or certain types of mental images (such as pictures of escaping, hurting what's hurting you, and so forth). Acceptance Two means you're not mentally resisting the experience. Of course, these two aren't literally different, but thinking about them this way can be helpful.

It's fortunate that there are two different types of acceptance available, because it gives you two different routes into the experience of acceptance. Even if your mind is filled with negative, difficult thoughts, you can often at least get your body to relax (Acceptance One). On the other hand, if your body is tensing up against something (usually pain, but also in disgust about something, etc.) you can find some acceptance in your thoughts about the object (Acceptance Two). Usually, if you can fire up one form of acceptance even a bit, the other one will eventually start coming online also.

When you begin to practice mindfulness, you will sometimes notice some repressed, denied, and uncomfortable thoughts and feelings coming up. It's not only a natural part of the practice; it's an important and useful feature. The goal is to bring this uncomfortable material out of the closet and expose it to the light of day. When psychological material is repressed, it controls you. It can make you reactive and take actions that you don't actually consciously want to do. This is not only true for things like denial of death, but also for difficult past experiences, traumas, and other things you'd rather not think about. When such things come up in meditation, which they sometimes will, the go-to action is to accept them. To relax and say, metaphorically if not literally, "Yes" to them. Not "Yes" as in they are OK, but "Yes" as in you recognize that they exist.

This is also the case for simple, physical pain. There was a woman in my meditation community, named Shirley, who had a truly awful spinal condition. Her vertebrae were growing spurs—growths like little knives made of bone—all over them in every direction. The spurs caused her terrible pain, pain so bad that the doctors installed a permanent morphine pump in her body. Shirley was experiencing an almost unimaginable level of pain (like an 11 on the 10 scale) 24 hours a day, for *decades*. There was literally nothing more she or any other human on earth could do to improve her medical condition. She just had to deal with it.

Once all external, physical fixes are exhausted, there remains only one thing to do: an internal, psychological fix: *acceptance*. Shirley in fact did this with great perseverance, and over time, became an expert meditator and facilitator of other meditators. She said that her practice of acceptance had greatly reduced the physical suffering she experienced, because she stopped fighting and resisting the pain all the time. Her acceptance really helped her situation, and reduced her suffering significantly.

Thankfully, most of us don't have to cope with such a difficult chronic pain condition, but all of us experience pain at some time. Meditation has been shown in several powerful studies to re-engineer your relationship to pain in a way that makes it much less difficult to bear. Mindfulness teaches you to feel your body sensations more accurately and completely, so you might think that that would make pain worse. And, indeed, fMRI studies show that long-term meditators do experience pain more completely—they are in essence meditating on the painful sensation, feeling it deeply. Non-meditators, on the other hand, show activation in the areas that suggest they are *thinking about* the pain. The paradoxical outcome of this is that the meditators actually have a much easier time bearing the pain. Why? Because they are not *resisting* it.[78]

Think of the tight fists, the stern repetition of the word, "NO." That's what resisting the pain is like. As with acceptance, there are two kinds of resistance: physical and psychological. Your body tends to tense up all around the painful area. Then you think thoughts about how unfair the pain is, how much you want to escape it, how much you do/don't deserve it, and so on. This is the mind resisting the pain. Both of these forms of resistance make the pain feel worse. You might think this is just some kind of mental game, sort of talking yourself out of the pain momentarily, but fMRI studies show that the pain experience is literally less intense.[79]

The teacher behind most of the methods in this book is Shinzen Young. He's a science nerd, a former math professor, and is a big fan of using pseudo-math equations to describe the principles of meditation. Shinzen has a bunch of formulas he uses to do that, but by far the most famous one points to the relationship between pain and resistance.

The equation is simple: $\mathbf{P} \times \mathbf{R} = \mathbf{S}$, or "pain times resistance equals suffering." This means that your level of suffering from pain is dependent upon how much you can let go of resisting it. In other words, relief from pain is all about how much you can accept the pain. Don't resist it, and you suffer much, much less. Japanese author Haruki Murakami has a famous quote, which sums up the situation nicely, "Pain is inevitable. Suffering is optional."

At first people are struck by the difference I'm making between pain and suffering. In everyday English, they are almost interchangeable. But here pain points toward the amount of negative physical stimulus, and suffering refers to your experience of that stimulus.

Pain is the objective aspect and suffering is the subjective aspect (if I can be a little imprecise about it).

Having done a lot of meditation on various sorts of pain, I can confirm that the formula (P x R = S) describes the basic situation. The more you let go of resistance, the less the pain hurts, so to speak. I remember one night having a questionable dinner, and then going home and erupting in an epic case of food poisoning. It was like Vesuvius at both ends, combined with vertiginous nausea, the shakes, fever, and moaning till dawn on the cold tile bathroom floor. By any measure, it was a miserable night.

At first I resisted this experience in every possible way. I tensed up against it. I hated it. I railed against it, the unfairness of getting sick, and so on. I fought it hard. Somewhere in the middle of the night, however, I remembered my training and made the effort to let go of all that resistance and start accepting the painful, negative sensations. After a short time I noticed that I wasn't really having such a bad time anymore. My body still felt very bad. My mind was still tired and unhappy. And yet, because I wasn't resisting it at all, it was all sort of "Meh, no big deal." I wouldn't call it a pleasant experience, but it was actually fairly neutral and not too hard to deal with. The next morning, I was done with that and moved on to other things. Enduring awful situations with a bit of sang-froid is one of the great boons of mindfulness.

Remember that by "accept" I don't mean that you believe that you deserve the pain, or that it's a good thing, or that you shouldn't palliate it given the chance. It's about relaxing and letting go of all resistance to the pain, whether that resistance is mental or physical. Let the pain be there, don't try to fight it. You may be surprised how effective this is.

It can also be a little terrifying at first. The tendency to tense up around pain can feel like it's somehow containing the pain, keeping it from spreading or getting worse. Of course, the tension doesn't actually do that, but when you first let go of it, it can feel scary, like the pain has been let out of its cage and it's going to get huge and spread everywhere.

Here's how you work with it. Let's say you're meditating on body sensation, and you're feeling some physical pain. If you want to work with it, begin meditating on the pain sensation. Notice it, label it, contact it deeply (and gently), and accept it completely. Let it be whatever it is. Concentrate on it, and examine its sensory qualities. Where it feels like it is, the physical extent of it, its three dimensional shape. And so on.

Focus mostly on the acceptance aspect. Don't try to change or control it. Don't manipulate it, resist it, or keep it at metaphoric arm's length. Get intimate with it. Physically relax around it as much as possible. Give it all the room in the world to be itself. If for whatever reason you just can't give up the resistance, then notice what the resistance feels like.

Emotional Acceptance

An even more common situation than physical pain is having negative emotions. Emotions like anxiety, worry, terror, depression, rage, frustration, and despair are just a part of everyday experience and will arise from time to time. I like to think of them as just another kind of pain, another part of the pleasure/pain guidance system given to us as human beings.

If you're feeling some of these when you sit down to meditate, and external distractions fall away, the difficult emotion you're feeling will well up and seem to be huge suddenly. Most of us spend energy suppressing emotions that we don't like, shoving them into our mental underground as much as possible.

Furthermore, we tend to believe that negative emotions are just wrong, a mistake, the result of some kind of injustice against us. We don't deserve to feel bad! We must've done something wrong. We're a bad person. We can then end up getting angry, anxious, or depressed about the bad feelings we're having. A spiral of negative emotions about the negative emotions.

One of the most common complaints I hear from meditation students is that they had a "bad meditation." Upon inquiry, it turns out that they experienced some negative emotions during sitting, and that's why it was "bad." Often, they had been looking forward to having a good meditation, and so they were also disappointed, angry, upset, ashamed, and/or guilty about the fact that they felt bad during meditation. Really, their "bad" meditation was a good meditation that simply felt unpleasant. True, meditation is supposed to improve your wellbeing, but that doesn't mean it will always improve your emotions during practice. It also doesn't mean that you will never feel bad. I'll discuss specific ways to deal with emotions in the coming chapters, but in this context, the important thing is to *simply accept them.*

Fighting everything all the time, resisting what's happening, creates a lot of needless stress. You can wear yourself out struggling against the inevitable, and stress is bad for you. At least during your meditation practice, if not at any other time during your day, let go of all this struggling. Let go of resistance. Relax, release tension, let go of the need to change everything. Say, "Yes" to experience. Breathe easy. Let everything just be the way it is right now, even if that's scary and it hurts. You'll feel better if you do.

CHAPTER FIFTEEN

Reach Out with Your Feelings

It's time for the Rebel Alliance to make their desperate attack on the Death Star. As Luke Skywalker rolls his X-wing fighter in toward the canyon-like surface of the battle station, the voice of Obi-Wan Kenobi speaks right into his head. "Luke, trust your feelings." Luke taps his earphones in confusion. Kenobi, after all, was recently killed by Darth Vader in an epic light saber duel.

After a few more urgings from the disembodied voice of Obi-Wan, Luke intuits that he doesn't need the X-wing's targeting computer in order to sink a pair of MG7-A proton torpedoes into the Death Star's unprotected thermal exhaust vent. Folding the computer away, Luke decides to use the Force and trust his feelings, and so (with some timely intervention from the *Millennium Falcon*) destroys the Empire's shiny new planet killer, moments before it can vaporize the rebel base on Yavin IV.

Although some would contest whether emotions are a good substitute for a targeting computer, it's interesting to ask what emotions actually *are* good for.[80] Most of us consider our emotions to be something inconvenient, something we're in conflict with, or are trying to manipulate to our benefit, or maybe something that gets in the way of our logical thinking.

Virtually everything you do every day you do in order to feel good emotionally. You date your partner to feel good, you work out to not feel bad. You earn money to not feel afraid of starving or to feel happy about the shiny products you line your nest with. And so on. Emotions rule your life. Based on that fact alone, understanding the background and function of emotions is clearly of supreme importance. The clearer picture you have of emotions, the clearer picture you have of your entire life, and mindfulness meditation is a very effective method for gaining clarity and insight about your emotions.

Human beings have long had a conflicted relationship with emotions. Philosophers and theologians have been almost uniformly negative in their view of emotions, which they named the "passions": something hot, irrational, wild, and uncontrollable within us. They compel us to do things that are embarrassing, dangerous, and irresistible. They are the drivers behind tragedy and make it "impossible to think," as Plato put it. For the Christian theologians, the passions were the cause of temptation, sin, and damnation, and for Buddhists, many emotions are delusional and poisonous, something to be strictly guarded against. Even early proto-scientific thinkers like Descartes and Spinoza felt that intense feelings were to be handled with care lest they overwhelm, degrade, and destroy a life. In short: thinking good, emotions bad.

This prejudiced view of emotions was retained to a large degree when science came into ascendance. "Men of rationality" continued to look down on the hysterical, unreliable, irrational emotions. Emotions were "feminine" and not to be trusted.

Despite Charles Darwin and William James each putting forth interesting (and largely correct) theories about them, emotions remained on the margins of respectable science well into the second half of the twentieth century. The behaviorists refused to acknowledge that they could be studied at all, and even cognitive psychologists were only able to approach emotions by seeing them as something cold, mental, and rational.

Looking at all this, you might say that humans have an irrational fear of emotions! So buckle up and get ready, because we're going to take a long, slow, clear look at these dangerous, slippery, fickle things called emotions. You'll even end up meditating on them as concrete physical experiences.

Evolutionary Guidance Systems

As we saw in the case of the fight-or-flight module of the human brain, certain emotional reactions have been highly conserved by evolution,[81] suggesting that they are vital components of animal survival. When you see similar structures and responses in a mouse that you do in a human being, you can bet that those structures and responses are pretty useful for staying alive.

As Darwin himself asserted in his bestselling book *The Expression of Emotion in Man and Animals* (1872), emotions in human beings didn't just arise out of thin air—they evolved from their animal precursors.[82] [83] From an evolutionary perspective of Darwin's Dharma, emotions evolved to help us survive and thrive, and they do this by motivating and directing our behaviors. That is, they act like a guidance system for the human organism.

An example of this is the emotion of fear. Let's say you're crossing the street, when suddenly you notice an 18-wheel semi truck roaring toward you at high speed. First of all, I feel it's my duty to warn you to never forget to look both ways before crossing the street. Second, you will likely experience an intense surge of fear. Organisms who didn't feel fear under similar dangerous conditions (even in the days before semi trucks) won the proverbial Darwin Award. They didn't become your ancestors. Therefore, almost all of us will feel afraid under these dangerous conditions. The surge of fear is a strong signal to *get out of the way right now.*

That's an example of your emotions functioning as they're supposed to—guiding your actions toward survival and wellbeing. Looking at emotions in this way instantly cuts through a lot of b.s. that you might tell yourself about what you're feeling. Feeling jealous about your love partner? Your emotional guidance system is trying to help you successfully reproduce. Feeling guilty about eating that last piece of pizza? Your emotional guidance system is trying to help you stay in the good graces of your in-group (and successfully reproduce). In this sense, your feelings are in line with Obi-Wan's after-death instructions to Luke to trust the guidance of his feelings instead of his computer. Your emotional guidance system has, after all, been around a lot longer than any system on an X-wing.

This way of looking at emotions is so useful that there is a short mnemonic I want you to use whenever you're trying to understand an emotion that you're experiencing: just say to yourself "guidance system." It forces you to look at an emotion for what it really is: an evolved response. In this sense, there's no such thing as a positive or negative emotion. They are all positive emotions, because they are part of the evolved human guidance system trying to get you to behave in a survival-enhancing manner.

I have to make an important warning here: I'm not saying that your emotions are correct or that you should always act on them. Most human evolution occurred a long time ago under very different conditions, so it's not that our emotional responses are necessarily good ones in the current environment. The example of Kim Nowak shows that our ancient drives are still in place in our brains, but out of place in society. Nowak is the former NASA astronaut who famously wore diapers on a long drive so she could (presumably) beat a romantic rival in the head. Clobbering the "other woman" in the Paleolithic would've won her the man, but trying to do it in modern Florida landed her in jail. The "guidance system" model isn't there to justify you doing whatever you feel like , or to follow every urge. Instead of saying that emotions are right, I'm saying that emotions are natural responses—not to be suppressed or denied, not something to feel guilty or ashamed about. If you wanted to be a little more accurate about it, you could call them an "ancient guidance system," one that may feel a little out of date or off the mark sometimes.

To go a little deeper into this way of understanding emotions, let's look at them one by one. The basic emotions are generally agreed to be fear, anger, sadness, disgust, and joy. (There are a surprising number of different lists.) They all shape our behavior in direct and specific ways. *Fear* gets you away from dangerous situations. *Anger* defends something you want, or drives away something you don't want. *Sadness* lets you know when you made a mistake, essentially saying, "Don't do that again." *Disgust* keeps you away from disease agents and poisons. *Joy* lets you know when you did something right, saying, "Do that again." These are evolved responses to motivate and direct us to make the most of various threats and opportunities.

What about more complex emotions such as guilt, shame, embarrassment, and pride? Human beings evolved for millions of years to function as part of a group, and these emotions are specifically for social situations, helping us to navigate our behavior with our clan, tribe, or in-group. *Guilt, shame,* and *embarrassment* are all slightly different, but they essentially say, "I'll never do that again" in a way that the whole group can read. Because the emotion plays a role in social interaction, it's important that those around us can actually see our embarrassment and grok that we are embarrassed. The skin flush is therefore a clear signal to everyone around us.

Pride, on the other hand, signals to the group that we did something right, and we're showing off how great we are. It's intended to up our status in the group, as well as to encourage group cohesion by showing what is correct or rewardable behavior. Pride displays are so hardwired into us that blind athletes who win at the Special Olympics do exactly the same arms up, chest puffed out gestures that their sighted compatriots do.

Besides actually inventing and expounding the theory of evolution, Darwin was the first to dig into the evolutionary view of emotions. By the 1950s, however, his evolutionary view of emotions had fallen into disfavor, mainly because theories based on genetics sounded too "Nazi" so soon after the war. Most scientists felt that emotional expressions were entirely culturally constructed—sort of a language each society invented and used to signal between members. Seen this way, emotions and emotional expressions should vary widely from culture to culture. Maybe people in other cultures laughed by farting, or something. But Paul Ekman, the researcher who the television fiction series *Lie to Me* was based on, demolished this view in the 1970s. He traveled to Borneo to gather support for the hypothesis that emotions were culturally determined. To his amazement, he found that people in Borneo understood all his emotional expressions, and he theirs, without any cultural translation. There seemed to be little or no difference between the emotional "language" of Americans and that of Borneans.

In the intervening years, this research has been supported and expanded considerably. Emotions, just as Darwin theorized, are part of our evolutionary heritage, and today we can back up this idea by looking at the relevant brain structures and neurochemistry. The amygdala, for example, which is involved in the fight-flight mechanism, and is similar in lower mammals and a human being. Nature nailed this brain network long ago, and it's been preserved in evolution and upgraded ever since. People don't culturally construct fear and aggression. These emotions—and all the others—are built into our biological machinery, part of the firmware. Emotions represent our biological inheritance from our ancestors, a sort of built-in survival guidebook.

In a way, emotions are like a more complex version of the advance-retreat mechanism at the base of the nervous system I described earlier. Big-name researchers like Joseph LeDoux and Richie Davidson have done a lot of work that supports this (although they usually call it "approach and avoidance" rather than advance-retreat). You could almost think of emotions as a second layer of that system, one that adds in a lot of complex behavioral and societal options specific to higher animals. And, like the pleasure/pain coding of the nervous system, emotions come in two basic flavors, pleasant and unpleasant.

Where There's a Positive...

Seeing emotions in their evolutionary context can really help you to understand how to work with them in your daily life. For example, a guidance system is useless if it is stuck on one setting. Imagine a compass needle that couldn't turn, or a maps app that only told you to turn right at every intersection. You need both north and south, right and left, as well as straight ahead, for a guidance system to function.

The same thing is true of your emotional guidance system. It won't work unless it has both a positive and a negative with which to motivate and direct you. Do this; don't do that. In other words, both pleasant and unpleasant emotions are absolutely necessary if the system is going to function. Having a clear understanding that both positive and negative feelings are natural, adaptive, and useful will go a long way toward engendering a sense of acceptance toward them.

This is bad news, if you were under the impression that—if you just made all the right decisions—someday you'd feel good all the time. This misconception is ubiquitous, and has been peddled from every corner of the ideological spectrum. Many people believe that it's possible and desirable for them to feel good all the time. Some religious beliefs around meditation claim that with enough practice you'll experience constant bliss and never feel bad. Some pharmacological corporations would like you to believe that if you take the right psych meds, you'll only ever feel happy. Even certain positive psychology systems sell the idea that, with the right combinations of thinking and imagining, you'll always feel just great.

If I were impolite, I would suggest that the idea that you were going to someday feel good all the time is a childish fantasy, which even the slightest scrutiny by a reasonable adult would reveal to be utterly non-viable. There are at least two problems with the glittering dream of permanent joy: (1) it couldn't work, and (2) you wouldn't like it if it did.

It's impossible to be permanently happy because the system always corrects itself. No matter how far you push the needle away from zero into the realm of super happiness, your biology will adjust and make that place the new zero. It's a self-adjusting, homeostatic system, and its tendency to return to a set-point is called "hedonic adaptation," or the "hedonic treadmill." (*Hedonic*, comes from the same root as "hedonism," and means to pursue pleasure.)

There are many examples of this phenomenon. One famous study concerns the happiness levels people from the two ends of the spectrum: lottery winners and victims of tragic accidents.[84] It would seem obvious that lottery winners would be happier than most people, and accident victims who lost the use of their limbs would be less happy than average. While both of these ideas were true for the first year or so after their life-changing events, after that their happiness level returns to whatever it was before the event.

Half of the study examined the fate of 22 lottery winners. The dream of winning big in the lottery caused Americans to spend over $65 billion in 2012. Yet the reality of winning doesn't deliver, because after a short time, the excitement of your new lifestyle wears off. It becomes the new norm, mundane. The small things you used to treasure, the little things in life that gave you pleasure previously, no longer do anything. Your emotional guidance system has adjusted to your new circumstances and migrated back to your original zero point.

The study also looked at paraplegics who had lost the use of their legs in tragic accidents. You may think that that would be the worst thing that could happen to you, and that you'd never feel happiness again. These victims did feel incredibly bad for as long as a year after their accidents. Yet even though they had permanently lost the ability to walk—a personal catastrophe by any measure—their hedonic system gradually adjusted, and after that, they were as happy as they had been before the accident.

How did this seeming miracle occur? The same way as with the lottery winners, but in reverse. Their brains adjusted to their new lifestyle, and they began to find pleasure in the simple things of life. In other words, their emotional guidance system had reset itself to zero, and they were back on track.

So it seems that no matter what you do, it's impossible to feel great, or awful, all the time. Whether your circumstances rise or fall, your brain will just adjust to that and make it the new normal. This has huge implications for acceptance, obviously. No matter what you're feeling right now, it's helpful to realize that it won't last.

Even if you could be happy all the time, it would be a very bad idea. Why? Because, much like little Roberto who can't feel pain, you would lose the ability to correctly navigate your life. The classic example of this is Phineas Gage, the man who, in 1848, was working as a highly respected and well-liked foreman on a railroad construction crew, when an explosion drove a metal rod clean through the front of his head. The accident severely damaged his frontal lobes, particularly the prefrontal cortex (PFC).

Although Gage recovered, he was never the same person afterward. His family and friends couldn't deal with him, and he lost his job on the railroad. He seemed unable to make decisions, couldn't control his emotions, drifted around working odd jobs, getting in fights, and eventually having to live with his mother.

Today we know that such behavior is indicative of damage to the prefrontal cortex of the brain. Modern researchers have looked into other people with damage to this area, often with similar difficulties. One of these unfortunate individuals, referred to in the medical literature simply as "Elliot,"[85] had lost parts of his prefrontal cortex when he had a brain tumor removed. Afterward, he was seemingly as before: charming, intelligent, and informed.

But Elliot lost the ability to make decisions. He would agonize endlessly over trivial decisions, but rush headlong and half-cocked into very important ones. Unable to hold a job, he squandered his money by making wildly unsound speculations, eighty-sixing his marriage in the process.

There are many other such cases, which demonstrate that damage to the PFC severely impairs the ability to make self-interested decisions, and leads to ruin. But why?

The PFC connects many different areas of the brain, including those concerned with reasoning and those concerned with sensing the feeling state of the body. When human beings go about making a decision, they collect data about the subject, much of which may be external and concrete, the kind of things cost-benefit analyses are made of. But that is not the whole story. We also consult memories of the past emotional states of the body, noting how we felt as the result of making similar decisions in the past. Most or all of this consideration goes on outside conscious awareness, but eventually the process gives rise to the feeling that one possibility is better than the rest. Even this feeling requires the ability to sense the emotions in the body,[86] and to coordinate this sensation with the decision-making function in the PFC.

The gist of all this is that *emotions are central to decision-making*. As much as we might like to imagine that we are calm and Spock-like in our choices, this is almost never the actual case. Although economic theory likes to assert that human beings are rational actors, studies have shown repeatedly that we are anything but. Somewhere under the hood, our emotional body sensations are playing a key role in every decision we make.

Neuroscientist and author Antonio Damasio calls one idea about how this works the "Somatic Marker Hypothesis," or SMH. To understand the SMH, you first have to understand that emotions are primarily somatic events—that is, we know we're having an emotion because we feel it in our body. This idea is usually a little weird for Westerners to accept; after 50 years of behavioral and cognitive psychology, we tend to think that these are primarily mental events. And while it's true that the brain is in charge of deciding, for example, that we should feel fear at the sight of an onrushing train, it makes this decision far below the level of conscious awareness. Furthermore, it triggers a whole series of bodily changes (faster heart rate and breathing, sweaty palms, energized limbs, etc.) that characterize the *feeling* of being afraid. Emotions may be orchestrated deep in the unconscious mind, but it is upon the *soma*—the feeling body—that their symphony is played out. In short: emotions are mainly embodied events.

Although we believe emotions are mental, the salient part of emotions actually occurs as sensations in your body. There is a fascinating study that demonstrates this in a very concrete way. Subjects who had received Botox treatments had blunted emotional responses to movie clips compared to people who had not received Botox.[87] Having your facial muscles (which are involved in the expression of emotions) paralyzed makes it harder to feel your own emotions. Furthermore, because we understand what other people are feeling by subtly mimicking their expressions, a second study showed that women who received Botox treatments had a much harder time empathizing with others.[88] A third study capitalized on this outcome by using a facial treatment that made the subject's muscles work harder to make expressions, which rendered them easier to feel. Sure enough, these people were much more accurate than controls at determining what others were feeling.[89]

So, emotions are mainly bodily (i.e. somatic) events, and you can learn to feel and track these events in your body sensation. Damasio hypothesizes that the brain uses such somatic markers to assist it in decision-making. These are memories of previous similar situations and the emotional tone associated with their outcome. As an example, you can imagine somebody trying to decide whether to buy a lottery ticket (rationally, always a bad idea). They may feel very excited about the possibility of winning, since the jackpot happens to be unusually huge. Yet, consciously or not, they remember feeling disappointed and downcast after all their previous attempts to win the lottery. This remembered emotional tone serves as a marker to aid in decision-making, guiding the person away from buying a ticket this time, because they remember (at least unconsciously) that they felt bad after all the other times they bought lottery tickets and failed to win.

Researchers devised a fascinating experiment to test this hypothesis. They created a game involving four decks of cards. Each deck contained cards that granted the participants actual money, or caused them to lose money. Two of the decks had a random number of positive and negative cards. But secretly, the other two decks were rigged to have many more negative cards than positive ones. This meant that some decks were "good," and would cause the subject to win money, and some were "bad," and would cause the subject to lose cash.

Healthy participants stopped choosing the bad decks after about 40 selections. Fascinatingly, they showed a stress response—as measured by changes in galvanic skin response—when choosing from the bad decks after only 10 draws, suggesting that their unconscious brain was *already aware* that these decks were no good. People with damage to the PFC, however, kept drawing from the bad decks as long as the game continued, meaning that they quickly went bankrupt and had to beg the researchers for additional funds. Furthermore, they did not exhibit a stress response to the bad decks—demonstrating that they did not have the emotions necessary to make good decisions.

Which brings me back to why you wouldn't actually want to feel happy all of the time. If emotions comprise a guidance system, a sort of compass to find your way in life, feeling only constant euphoria would be like sticking a huge magnet to the side of the compass. You would lose all ability to tell direction. Every decision would seem just wonderful, and you would soon end up deep in a ditch. Evolution has "figured this out" and created a system that constantly resets our emotional baseline to zero, whatever our circumstances. That way, we always have a useful and functional emotional guidance system at work in our lives.

This is also a big reason why taking drugs and alcohol can be so damaging. Besides the physical problems they can create, they lead to poor decision-making. We're taking them is to manipulate our emotions, to monkey with our emotional tone, but it also screws up our decision-making process.

Thus you cannot feel happy all the time, and it would actually be bad if you did. Imagine if Luke folded away his targeting computer and trusted his feelings to destroy the Death Star while he was immersed in a sea of bliss. He'd probably just skip off in space somewhere, giggling like a newbie stoner. The fantasy that when you have a better job, find the right partner, buy the right car or home, have a baby, or when you (fill in the blank), you'll finally live happily ever after is simply not true. You may find these things satisfying, and they can contribute to your quality of life, but they'll not make your emotional tone change to a permanent or even abnormally high state of happiness. You will adjust and that will become your new normal, and—at least in terms of emotion—you will be back to zero. And that's a very good thing.

Finding Flexibility

All of the biological and evolutionary background of emotions and emotional responses leads to one big conclusion: it's a good idea to accept your emotions as they are. First, see that most or all of your behavior every day is directed toward doing things that you think will make you feel good, or removing things that you think are making you feel bad. In other words, notice that you are utterly controlled in virtually every moment by your emotions. Even if you think that you're doing something that you don't like because it's a moral, positive, correct, or rational thing to do, deep down, you're getting an emotional reward for doing it.

Second, recognize that human emotions are responses that were programmed into our biology over millions of years. We like to think that our emotions are personal, intimate, and special things about us, but actually, they are largely mechanistic and programmatic. Yes, human beings are so complex that we can have very unpredictable and individual responses. But recognizing that the emotions you're feeling are not necessarily "yours" as much as they are a reaction is very useful.

Admitting this means that you can stop taking so much personal responsibility for every little thing you are feeling. Not every emotion you are having is one that you decided to have, especially not consciously. Taking personal responsibility for your emotions makes about as much sense as taking personal responsibility for aspects of your liver function. Instead, accept that you're feeling how you're feeling. If you want to change it later, you can try to do that. If you want to let go of habits that are making you feel bad, you can do that, too. But beating yourself up for how you are feeling at this moment is counterproductive.

Third—and this is the big one—feeling bad doesn't always mean that there's something wrong with you, or that you did something wrong. We as a society are very intolerant (resistant, even) to the presence of unpleasant emotions. If you're feeling bad, something is terribly wrong and we rush to fix it immediately. We do this even when the feeling response makes perfect sense. For example, Americans even take antidepressants after the death of a loved one, because the grief can be so intense. During the recent updating of the DSM-IV—the manual psychiatrists use to diagnose patients—they wanted to categorize grief as a mental illness! A suggestion that was thankfully vetoed. Grief feels very unpleasant, it's true, but is that negative feeling actually a problem? Isn't it a completely natural response to feel grief after someone you love dies? Would you want to somehow not feel it?

When we see emotions in this light, we can begin to have an entirely different relationship to them. You start to understand that they are simply happening, like your heartbeat or your breathing. They are there to guide your behavior, not to make you feel good.

It's possible to take this concept too far, however. If you are experiencing clinical depression, anxiety disorder, or some other emotional malfunction, for example, taking a psychopharmacological medication could be an important step in your return to wellbeing. Getting your emotional system in good working order is crucial, and sometimes the process requires medicine, psychotherapy, and other interventions.

In mindfulness meditation, however, the main way that we will work with emotions is to both accept them, and to try and acquire a great deal of sensory clarity about them. Acceptance I've already described, and the sensory clarity aspect we've worked with to some degree. You will learn to be very precise, detailed, and specific with regard to emotional sensations.

When I describe this form of meditation, it's common to get the response, "Why should I do that?" But I can assure you that it's a powerful and helpful technique, and there is a good deal of science to back me up. Meditating on emotions in the body will, like other body sensation meditations, develop your insula,[90] which is that part of your brain that is associated with (among other things) the feeling of visceral sensations. Body meditation practice will help you get better at sensing such sensations over time, something that Shinzen calls "skill at feeling."[91] Skill at feeling has a number of important benefits. One is that it will give you a better and better look at how you're feeling. Many people have a difficult time describing what they're actually experiencing emotionally. It's not so much a lack of vocabulary, but a lack of the ability to contact emotional sensations with clarity. They just know that they're feeling something. By developing skill at feeling, you will have a much better idea of what you're experiencing at any moment in time. Given that emotions are so important in decision-making, being able to feel them more clearly could be very helpful in making good decisions.

Not only will you know better what you're feeling, but you'll get a much better idea what other people are feeling. As I mentioned, we tune into other peoples' feelings by subtly mimicking their expressions in our own faces as "microexpressions." We are normally not consciously aware that we are doing this. It's part of our built-in mechanism for working together in a group of hominids, as our ancestors have done for a very long time indeed. Meditating on emotional sensations begins slowly to make the feelings of these microexpressions noticeable, which—much like in the experiment mentioned above—makes it much easier to accurately read what other people are feeling. That's a crucial skill for deepening connection with others, which builds not only relationships, but also resilience—the ability to recover after difficult experiences.[92]

Viktor Frankl—the neurologist, psychologist, and Auschwitz survivor—once wrote that "Between stimulus and response there is a space. In that space is our power to choose our response. In our response lies our growth and our freedom." This brilliant quote points to one of the deepest and most important benefits derived from meditating on the emotions: it increases your behavioral flexibility. Human beings display a surprising amount of automaticity in their behavior; that is, under the same conditions, we tend to do the same things over and over again. Regardless of whether the behavior is effective or desirable, we automatically repeat it with a kind of mechanical predictability. To put it in Frankl's terms, there is no distance between stimulus and response. For the same stimulus, you get the same response, every time.

Meditating on the emotions, however, does something very interesting: it builds a kind of gap, or as Frankl puts it, a "space" between the stimulus and the response. It's hard to describe, but it's something that's shockingly obvious the first time you experience it.

There will be, for example, a loud BANG!, and you expect yourself to jump. But instead, it's like an hour goes by and you're still waiting for the jump to happen. It does, eventually, but only after you've had plenty of time to consider it.

By cultivating this space between stimulus and response, you gain something every human being ever born has wanted: the ability to choose whether to respond to an emotional urge or not. The emotions haven't changed; you're not submerging yourself in some numbing sea of bliss. Instead, you feel everything very keenly, but have the ability to *not act on it if you don't want to.*

Think of all the times you've done something rash and regretted it afterward. Said something out of rage or spite that should never have been spoken. Think of all the urges, maybe even compulsions or addictions that you automatically respond to, even when you don't want to. Meditation on emotions allows you to gain some measure of control; one might even dare to say wisdom, with respect to the expression of emotions. You are able to respond, rather than simply react.

This is such a life-changer that it's hard to exaggerate its usefulness. There is, of course, a reason that all those ancient philosophers and theologians were so negative about the passions. It's so easy for a human being to do something terrible and irreversible in a moment of emotional intensity, and then to regret it for the rest of their lives. Meditation on emotion can help to make sure that you think before you act.

Feeling Emotion in the Body

Let's talk about how to actually do the practice called Focus on Emotion. Just like the Focus on Relaxation technique, Focus on Emotion is about contacting a subset of general body sensations. In this case, the subset is composed of sensations that "feel emotional."

Feeling emotions in the body, in a precise and continuous manner, is the goal of the practice.

When I first describe this technique, people tend to imagine that emotional body sensations are something really special, or something really large. Usually they are neither. Most of the time, emotional body sensations are pretty subtle and normal. The trick is learning to separate them out from all the other sensations going on, to extract the signal from the noise.

Let's begin with a little taste of how this works. If you are alone right now, and nobody is watching you, make a big smile on your face. It doesn't matter how fake it is, just instruct your face muscles to generate the features of a smile.

Now, bring your awareness into contact with the sensations in your face around the smile. You can feel some rather large physical changes in your muscles. The corners of the lips pull up, the cheeks bunch up, the lips themselves thin out, and so on. Tune into the sensation of all this muscle activity, and the feelings in the skin around it. Rack through a few reps of the meditation algorithm on these sensations. Get really clear about how they feel.

Next, take it further, into something a bit subtler. See if you can feel, in your face, the slightly pleasurable or pleasant sensation associated with the smile. For most people, this can be very subtle at first. It's not big, obvious, or brash, just a small sense of pleasure that comes from smiling. This sensation—no matter how small—is also a major component of the emotional experience in the body. Use your meditation algorithm on the sensations in your face, attempting to feel this pleasant smile sensation as clearly as you can.

Now feel both things at the same time: the gross sensations in the muscles, skin, and flesh, and the subtler pleasant sensations. You can either contact one at a time, pendulating back and forth between them, or contact both at the same time, using a larger area of focus. Stick with this for a minute or so.

These sensations are one example of contacting emotion in the body; in this case, the emotion is joy. You may feel that such a small, insignificant pleasant sensation in your face—if you were even able to contact it at first, and some people aren't—is much too mundane to be called anything as substantive as joy. But it's just a matter of degree. There are smaller or larger amounts of joy possible, but it's all the joy response, just the same.

Many people also reject the idea that simply making this mask of a smile has any relationship to real joy, however small. But my experience is that it absolutely does, and science backs this up neatly. Experimenters in the 1970s attached electrodes to the faces of subjects reading cartoons. The electrodes forced the faces of the subjects into smiles (using a cover story about measuring muscle activity) and then had them rate how funny they thought the cartoons were. Subjects whose faces had been electrically forced into a smile thought the cartoons were funnier—presumably because they were smiling physically, and this generated the pleasant smile feeling.

This experiment was reengineered in the 1980s by Strack into something much more elegant.[93] He had subjects rating the humor value of cartoons, as before, but manipulated their facial muscles by asking them to hold a pencil in their teeth. There were two ways to hold the pencil, one that caused a smile and one which caused a frown. In this case, too, subjects who held the pencil in a way that caused a mechanical smile rated the humor value of the cartoons significantly higher. And those who were tricked into frowning in this manner found the cartoons much less funny.

So even creating the mechanical approximation of an emotional response can generate a measurable change in how you feel emotionally. Even if the reason is unconscious (which it probably was in the above experiments), your system responds like it's a "real" emotion. I would contend that it is a real emotion, just one that's being stimulated from the other end—the tail wagging the dog.

I lived in Los Angeles for a long time, and many of my students there were actors. They often remarked how closely this idea matched the "method acting" techniques they learn in acting classes. By putting your body in posture of anger, and making the facial expressions of anger, you will end up feeling angry, for example.

The Focus on Emotion technique reverse engineers this, in a way. The idea here is that by very closely monitoring subtle emotional expressions in the face and body, you can understand what you're thinking and feeling with much greater clarity. Given the utter centrality of emotions to our daily sense of wellbeing, it should be no surprise that cultivating this sort of skill with regard to feeling emotions is so effective.

FOCUS ON EMOTION — GUIDED TECHNIQUE

Before you begin, find your meditation seat, either sitting in a chair, on a bench, cushion, or on the floor.

Sit up straight, extending your spine upwards toward the ceiling. Make sure your chin is pointing just slightly (5 degrees) below horizontal.

Next, relax your entire body. Take three deep breaths, and let each one of them out long and slowly.

Now you're ready to begin the Focus on Emotion practice.

Scan your face for any emotional body sensations. These could take the form of scowls, smiles, furrowed brows, or other small muscle contractions. It could even be the case that you just "feel some emotion" there, without being entirely sure why. Bring your meditation algorithm to bear on these emotional body sensations. The label you can use is "emotion." Contact the emotional sensation deeply, be as specific as possible about what you feel there, and try to accept whatever it is.

If there are no emotional sensations present, that's fine. Still meditate on the body sensations in your face region for a little while. The label you can use is "none," meaning no emotional sensations. If, while you're doing this, an emotional sensation arises, focus on that, and switch to using the label "emotion."

Move on to the throat region, and scan for any emotional body sensations. If you find any, focus on them using the meditation algorithm and the label "emotion." If you don't find any, focus on the lack of emotional sensation for a shorter time, using the label "none."

Move on to the chest region, and scan for emotional sensations. This can be a particularly rich zone for emotions.

As you're working your meditation algorithm in any of these regions, make sure to emphasize the acceptance aspect with regard to emotional sensations. Whatever emotions you're feeling are fine in this moment. Even if they are unpleasant or upsetting, just let them be whatever they are. Try not to resist or to struggle with them.

Move on to the belly region, and scan for emotional body sensations. This can also be a strong area for emotions.

Now scan your whole body for emotional sensations.

You can stop here, or go back to a region of particularly intense or interesting emotional body sensations and work with that for a longer time.

When it's time to finish, spend at least one minute just sitting quietly, meditating on relaxed sensations in the body before continuing on your day.

❀

CHAPTER SIXTEEN

Coping with Too Much Feeling

In the movie *Blade Runner*, the replicant Roy Batty, played by Rutger Hauer, has a problem. As a genetically enhanced human-like Nexus 6 organism, he's been given a brilliant mind and a super-human body by the Tyrell Corporation that created him. He is used to performing dangerous and difficult work in space and on off-world colonies. Yet to keep him and others like him under control, the replicants have a built-in four-year lifespan limit. Batty and his replicant friends—Pris, Leon, and Zhora—are programmed to die any day now, and they're not too happy about it. In a desperate attempt to extend their lives, the four replicants illegally travel to Earth, in search of somebody who can help them.

Although Roy is a genius, he is still like a three year old child emotionally. The feelings of fear and outrage he is experiencing are enormous, and he cannot deal with them. When he faces the head of the Tyrell Corporation, his creator, he angrily demands "more life, fucker." When Tyrell makes it clear that there is no possible way to do that, Roy is overcome with anger and frustration and kills the man with his bare hands.

As all of his friends are killed, his overwhelming feelings push Roy to more and more extremes. Yet at the very end, worn out and dying,

Roy comes to some kind of acceptance of his situation, and speaks hauntingly of the beauty he has seen in his short life.

In most mindfulness meditation, the idea is to accept what you're feeling, and to greet all emotions with curiosity, openness, and nonjudgment. Even if they are painful and negative, you investigate them in detail. Sometimes, however, digging directly into a big, difficult emotion just isn't possible or desirable—it might be too gnarly to deal with effectively, like in Roy Batty's situation. Rather than meditating on the waves of emotion breaking on the beach of awareness, it's more like a tsunami of feeling obliterating the beach.

This can happen for a number of reasons. If you have experienced trauma, it's common for certain situations to trigger overwhelming feelings. If you are under an unusually large amount of stress, say losing a job or a big housing change, it's possible that your emotions could feel much more difficult to cope with. Another possibility is that you are experiencing chronic anxiety or depression, and connecting with the core of these feelings starts a feedback loop that spirals out of control.

Whatever the cause, emotional overwhelm can feel like it's going to make you crazy, cut you in half, tear you apart, or even kill you. You might feel like you cannot bear another second of it, and that nothing can relieve it. Emotional overwhelm sucks, and it's not a good place to hang out.

It can also make you dissociate. Dissociation happens when the feelings are so bad that you cannot bear to feel your body anymore at all, and you, metaphorically, "leave your body." That means to lose direct conscious contact with most body sensations. It's a common response for people who have PTSD. Dissociation feels like spacing out, blanking out, being half in a trance, or slightly on drugs. And in a way that's exactly what it is. The overwhelm feels so bad that you're checking out—usually into some mental activity—in order to avoid feeling it.

Hopefully these are not common occurrences in your life, but they do happen to all of us sometime, and it's important to know how to cope. In all of these cases, meditating directly on the intense feelings of emotion in the body may not be the best course of action. It's good to connect with your feelings under normal conditions, but wading directly into an enormous flood of emotion that threatens to drown you is not recommended.

There are two basic strategies for working with overwhelming emotions in the body: focus on a neutral spot in the body, or focus on something external.

Focus on a Neutral Spot

Although emotional sensations can arise anywhere in the body, they are much more likely to arise in the belly, chest, throat, or face. These are the emotional hotspots in the body, the regions where emotional sensations can get huge. That means that other areas are much less likely to host gigantic emotional sensations, which turns out to be a useful and convenient thing. You can meditate on those emotionally "cold" spots, such as your hands and feet, and stay in touch with your body. As long as you're in touch with your body, you won't be completely dissociated. You'll be anchored in the sensations, rather than checked out into a dream-like state. And since the emotional sensations in these locations are typically much smaller or nonexistent, you won't be overwhelmed either.

The easiest practice is to feel your hands, your feet, or both. Concentrate on the emotionally neutral sensations in these areas. For example, explore the sensations in your palms, the back of your hand, each of your fingers, the spaces between the fingers, and so on. Even your arms and legs, if they are not filled with too much emotional sensation. Contact as much of the body as is "safe"—meaning areas not filled with overwhelming feelings.

Intense emotions can be seductive, even if they are unpleasant. They are like whirlpools that suck your attention toward them, so avoid allowing yourself to be drawn into the emotional hotspots. Just stay focused on your hands and feet. This is an effective way to work with big feelings.

Focus on Something External

When the body is too emotionally hot, a second good idea is to meditate on something outside the body. External sights and sounds are powerful meditation objects, especially when they are interesting, beautiful, or compelling in some way.

I remember one time when I was going through a terrible relationship breakup. It felt like I had no center, and my guts were dragging on the ground. The feelings were so large and so negative that I didn't feel I could deal with them for another second.

I knew that one possibility for working with such intense feelings was focusing away from them. Looking up, I noticed a large cumulous cloud over the nearby mountain. It was stunningly white against the penetrating blue of the sky. It seemed to be a mountain itself, composed of voluminous floating marble. The beauty of it really captured my attention. I began to meditate on it. Staying open and curious and exploring it visually. Every little detail.

Then the horrendous feelings would pull me in again, but I simply accepted that. I didn't fight it at all. As soon as I could, with a lot of relaxation and openness, I just brought my attention back to the beauty of the cloud. Because I love painting, drawing, and photography, and have developed an aesthetic eye, I knew to concentrate on the details of color and shape, and that helped in staying focused on the cloud.

That cloud saved me. It gave me something to place my attention on that was safe and pleasant and emotionally neutral. You can do something similar with music, although the caveat is to not use music that is too emotionally stimulating.

Pendulation

I said that there were two techniques, but I'll toss in a third for free. It's called pendulation, and it's slightly more difficult than the above techniques. It often takes some previous experience of focusing on a neutral spot. If you can do pendulation, however, it's worth it.

To pendulate, you first locate an emotional-neutral spot in the body and meditate on it for a little while. The next step is the tough one. If you have a huge emotion occurring, but you think you can contact it, or contact somewhere near it, without getting totally overwhelmed, then do that. Contact some part of the huge emotion and meditate on that for a very brief time. If you feel yourself getting overwhelmed, immediately come back to the neutral spot.

Then you continue to go back and forth (i.e. pendulate) between the neutral spot and the emotional hotspot. You concentrate on only one at a time, giving it your complete attention. Neutral — Hotspot — Neutral — Hotspot… back and forth for the entirety of the meditation.

Going back and forth like this is tremendously integrating. It sort of allows the two different spots in the body to "talk" to each other. Eventually, the emotional hotspot may calm down a bit. It's important to remember that you're not trying to make it calm down, or force it to be neutral. You're practicing acceptance with it. But nevertheless it may sometimes become markedly less intense.

Pendulation is so effective that it's the core practice of several PTSD treatments. For example, the work of Bessel van der Kolk and Peter Levine use something comparable (although not exactly the same). Of course, if you have PTSD or other intense traumatic reactions happening, you'll want to get professional help to work it through

CHAPTER SEVENTEEN

Meditation and Meaning

"Life is without meaning. You bring the meaning to it. The meaning of life is whatever you ascribe it to be. Being alive is the meaning."

~ Joseph Campbell

If you Google the phrase "meaninglessness of life," you'll get almost half a million hits. Quotes from great thinkers and pages from philosophy sites all wrestle with the human sense that everything is for nothing and life is absurd. The haunting lines uttered by Matthew McConaughey's character Rust Cohle in the epic first season of the TV show *True Detective* captivated viewers by explicitly pointing out our collective pain at this sense of meaningless.[94]

The promise of *The Mindful Geek* is that it will help you to find wellbeing through the practice of mindfulness meditation. But can we really have wellbeing while drowning in a sea of meaninglessness?

Psychologist Martin Seligman, a founder of the positive psychology movement, wrote the bestselling book *Authentic Happiness* about how to find happiness in life. Despite its popularity, however, in the face of criticism and his own developing understanding, Seligman realized that happiness, which is a transient emotional state, may not be a beneficial goal of life. "Doing what make me happy," moment-by-moment could mean becoming a slave to every passing whim, no matter how immoral, illegal, or destructive, as long as it made you happy. What if you never went to work, never washed, or never learned anything new because it was hard and didn't make you happy?

As he explains in his 2011 book *Flourishing*, Seligman worked hard to revise the definition of a positive psychology goal to make more sense to an adult trying to have a "good life." He created a five-part definition of "flourishing," dubbed PERMA, and posits these five qualities:

- Positive emotions
- Engagement
- Relationships
- Meaning, and
- Accomplishments.

Positive emotions — means having at least some ability to feel happiness, but also qualities such as interest, excitement, awe, and pride.

Engagement — is Seligman's way of talking about a flow state, when we are absorbed in doing things we find intrinsically interesting.

Relationships — probably the most important driver of wellbeing is having family, friends, lovers, and other people to do things with.

Meaning — feeling that what you are doing is important, worth doing, interesting, and contributes to the greater good is vital.

Accomplishments — human beings find joy in pursuing success and mastery, even if it causes some difficulty and stress.

This formulation represents a more fully considered and powerful view of wellbeing than the simplistic phrase "being happy." It includes the fact that activities like raising children may not make a person "happy"—most studies show that people's happiness is actually reduced while child rearing—yet still contribute massively to a sense of wellbeing and having a life well-lived.

Most of the PERMA factors are covered elsewhere in this book. Engagement, as I mentioned, can be thought of as a synonym for concentration and flow. Meditation can help you to have better relationships with people, and to help create the conditions for greater accomplishment.

Meaning, according to Seligman, is the one factor that puts the other four into perspective and gives them a context. Without meaning, the other parts of wellbeing ring hollow. Even if the world is meaningless, as Joseph Campbell asserts in the quote at the beginning of this chapter, it is possible for us to create our own meaning.

It's hard to overestimate the benefit to your wellbeing of profoundly tapping into a sense that there's something you really value in this world. The sense that—even if in the Grand Scheme of Things it's all meaningless—there is still something that is *very meaningful to you.* Something that is important to you, and that you feel good about putting all your effort into. Even Rust Cohle seemed to find meaning at the very end of his cold-case hunt for a serial killer.

Meditation can do a lot to overcome this sense of meaninglessness. At its best, it can begin to infuse your life with a tangible sense of real meaning and purpose. Mindfulness is an excellent, concrete practice you can work with to find what is meaningful to you. The key is to remember that emotions are not in your head, they are embodied experiences. We may think of meaning as being mental or conceptual, but it is through the feelings in your body that you discover where meaning exists for you. What tugs at your heart.

I remember my early days of meditating on emotions. One time I went to work, like on any other day, and ran into a coworker at the water cooler. Like every other morning, we exchanged pleasantries, but this time something was different. Because I had been meditating on emotional body sensations just an hour or so earlier, I was still quite tuned into what I was feeling. And I noticed, as I spoke with my colleague, that subtle sensations of discomfort, dislike, and even anger were arising. These were so faint and in the background that I'm sure even a week earlier, I wouldn't have been able to detect them. They were extremely subtle. But now I could not only feel them, I couldn't ignore them. I took them as a wake up call to examine my relationship with this person more closely.

Sure enough, I realized that we were getting involved in some negative behaviors with each other—typical difficult coworker stuff—but that it was still so early in the process that it hadn't reached the level of explicit manifestation yet. It had all been going on under the hood until that moment. Given this early warning, I was able to take actions to smooth out our relationship, and after that we were fine. But I never forgot how the practice of mindfulness meditation had given me heightened sensitivity to my own feelings, and that allowed an almost prescient sensitivity to my interactions with others.

As you meditate on body sensations, you eventually get better at knowing what you're feeling. This is not only true in the sense of resolving unclarity about feelings, but also in the sense of becoming able to detect feelings at subtler levels. It's possible to almost know "in advance" what you're going to feel about something. This is not literal prediction, but rather you're able to detect the faint stirrings of emotion about a topic or experience far sooner than you would have been able to previously. It almost feels like a kind of radar or early warning system for feelings. The normal everyday word for this capacity is *intuition*. It's about becoming clearer about your own gut feelings. Intuition is not magic. It is eminently trainable and can be cultivated on purpose, using meditation.

Being able to better contact what you're feeling can also work in a positive situation—it can help you to detect when you like something or someone even a little bit. And knowing what excites you, what turns you on, what makes you feel good is extremely important information to have, even if it is very subtle.

The problem for many of us is that when we hear someone say something like, "Follow your bliss" (another Joseph Campbell quote, BTW), we operate under the assumption that the bliss is going to be huge. Like some mixture of an orgasm, candy flipping, and a *My Little Pony: Friendship Is Magic* episode. Let there be joy and rainbow Skittles squirting from every orifice! Good for you if going to work feels like that (and good luck getting anything done), but for most of us, the bliss Joseph Campbell is talking about is much less extreme than that. It's more like a slightly warm, expansive feeling in the chest, a subtle glow around the smile, or a mild spring in the step. The sense that it feels good to do what you're doing; maybe the sense that it *matters*.

Without explicit training in contacting emotional sensations, these little hints of excitement might just stay hidden under the hood. You would simply have some unconscious urges that didn't end up meaning very much. But once you can detect these sensations, you can tune into the explicit guidance they are offering you. They point toward something that is indispensable in life: knowing what you value.

Many of us have a list of things we can rattle off at will if somebody asks us about what we love or what we think is important. But when did you make that list, and when was the last time you checked to see if it was still true? Do you really feel that passionately about the things you did ten years ago? Did you ever really care about it, or did it just seem like the right thing to care about? The only way to know is to think about it and *feel what happens in your body*. If the feeling of excitement, energy, or a tingling sensation is there, that is the sign that you still find this important. If not—or if you actually feel some subtle deflation, let down, or even negative feelings—maybe your interest in it is taking a momentary break, or you've moved on to other things. Give yourself the room to change, grow, and discover new interests. There's no law that what is meaningful to you has to stay the same from day to day, year to year.

When new meditation students begin working with me, I sometimes jokingly say that meditation "will destroy your life." I'm mostly kidding, but in another way, I'm completely serious. Meditation won't actually destroy your life; of course, it will help you to fix your life. It will likely help you live a life that is more meaningful and fulfilling for you. By tuning into your actual feelings about the activities, people, environments, and situations with which you interact, meditation is an extremely potent way to decide what works for you and what doesn't.

The joke I'm making is that when they start meditating, many people soon realize, for example, that they're in completely the wrong relationship, a job that doesn't suit them, or they're in an intolerable living situation. This incompatibility was flying below the radar previously, but becomes blatantly obvious once meditation starts generating insights. It's not uncommon for a person who has been meditating for six months to a year to be going through a relationship breakup and looking for a new job. In fact, it's so typical that it's one of the reasons I feel it's important to write this chapter.

Before you start working with this practice, important information about your life—how you feel about various things—is below your level of conscious awareness. As you deepen your practice, much of that information will become consciously available to you. Nothing could be more valuable. You could be saving years of your life that would've otherwise been frittered away. You are saving your time and energy, and the time and energy of others around you. You are getting yourself on track. As we've been discussing, our emotions are a kind of guidance system, and as you target them with more sensitivity, they can become the equivalent of an early-warning system. Not only can you shed current situations that are not right for you, you can *avoid* getting into ill-fitting situations in the future.

This isn't always easy. It's common to try to talk yourself out of this intuitive form of knowing, using all the rational, logical, verbal skills at your command. It also takes a lot of courage to act. Sometimes knowing, for example, that a relationship isn't right for you means that you have to face some very uncomfortable and even painful conversations.

In the long run, however, this is the road to finding meaning. Sometimes people react negatively when I use the word "meaning." They associate it with some sort of pre-programmed or dogmatic system that tells you what you are supposed to find meaningful. As you can see, that's not what we're doing here.

Meaning, as Campbell suggests, is something you create for yourself. But it's not always so easy. It's not as if a light bulb appears above your head, the room fills with light, and you announce that you've found the reason for your existence.

If you want to try get in touch with some meaning right now, it's easy to do. Sit in meditation, relax, and get comfortable. Then bring to mind things that you found meaningful in the past. Do this one at a time, very slowly. As you think of one, search for emotional body sensations about it. Don't be surprised if there aren't any, or the ones that arise are not what you expected them to be. It's extremely important not to judge whatever comes up.

Next bring to mind things that you have found meaningful recently. If you don't know of any, think of whatever activities you've been spending time doing. Notice whatever emotional sensations occur surrounding each one.

There may be all sorts of different emotional sensations about any particular activity, but the one you should be on the lookout for is excitement, interest, "energy," or joy. Again, these may be very subtle, but regardless, they signal something that is meaningful for you right now.

Once you've done this, what do you do with the information? Sometimes it's enough to just know. But it can be helpful to realize that this is your emotional guidance system performing its orienting function. It's pointing you in the direction of what matters to you. The hope is that you will then prioritize that activity, engage with it more fully and more often.

As you practice this more frequently, and act upon what you discover, you'll find your life taking some surprising turns. Turns in the direction of greater wellbeing and a greater sense of purpose. Enjoy.

CHAPTER EIGHTEEN

Concentration and Flow

Ray Bradbury, the author of such science fiction classics as *The Martian Chronicles* and *The Illustrated Man*, needed a quiet place to write. He was a young author with a couple of squalling toddlers at home and no money to rent an office. He searched until he wandered into the Lawrence Clark Powell Library at UCLA and heard the sound of typewriters. Following the sound down into the basement, he found a room with nine or ten students frantically typing away. For just ten cents, you could rent a typewriter for a half hour.

Going to the bank and getting a bag of dimes, he returned, put ten cents into the slot, and started writing. Bradbury was trying to support his family as a young writer, and even 10 cents was a lot of money. He had to write as a fast as possible, cram as much into his 30 minutes as possible—the original NaNoWriMo. Between bouts of finger bashing, he'd wander the UCLA stacks, reading books and dreaming of what to put into his manuscript next. Nine dollars and eighty cents later he pulled the last page of his finished novel from the machine. He recalled feeling that the flow of time had accelerated, and the novel, with the odd title *Fahrenheit 451*, had just sort of written itself.[95]

Have you ever been so involved in doing something that the rest of the world seemed to disappear? Or time slowed down, you felt wonderful, and even your sense of self disappeared? The great Brazilian soccer star Pele talked about an experience in which he felt:

"...a strange calmness I hadn't experienced in any of the other games. It was a type of euphoria; I felt I could run all day without tiring, that I could dribble through any of their teams or all of them, that I could almost pass through them physically. I felt I could not be hurt."[96]

You might think that such an experience has to do with performance-enhancing drugs, or perhaps calling upon your mutant superpowers, but actually it's the result of nothing more exotic than *concentration*. Hungarian psychologist Mihaly Csikszentmihalyi— basically the living god of concentration theory—looked at people doing different activities in a state of high concentration, and found that they were generally calm, relaxed, open, and felt very good. Whether they were writing poetry, composing music, playing sports, doing math, or whatever else, they wanted to continue concentrating as long as they could, and they wanted to return to it as often as possible. Even if the activity they were doing had no external rewards like money or prestige, they felt that it was worth doing for its own sake because it felt so good. If the concentration state went even deeper, time seemed to slow down or stop, and the sense of self diminished or disappeared, with only the sense of pleasurable and total involvement in the activity remaining.

One of the best parts of his work is his extensive library of quotes from highly creative people talking about their experiences. For example, one (unnamed) American composer described it like this:
"You are in an ecstatic state to such a point that you feel as though you almost don't exist. I have experienced this time and again. My hand seems devoid of myself, and I have nothing to do with what is happening. I just sit there watching it in a state of awe and wonderment. And [the music] just flows out of itself."

Csikszentmihalyi noticed that people kept describing this state using phrases like "effortless flow" or "spontaneous flow," so he dubbed it, "flow," and has dedicated decades of research to its study. Other common terms for flow include being "in the zone," "in the groove," "in the pocket," and others. As Csikszentmihalyi defined it, flow is "being completely involved in an activity for its own sake.[97] The ego falls away. Time flies. Every action, movement, and thought follows inevitably from the previous one, like playing jazz. Your whole being is involved, and you're using your skills to the utmost."

That sounds pretty mystical, but it's actually totally normal, even mundane. We all get into a light flow state at least some of the time. A typical example of a flow state would be a crossword puzzle enthusiast focused on filling in the squares. She becomes calm and relaxed, and yet is very alert and engaged in the process. As she searches for the answers to the clues, she blots out everything else happening around her. She may not hear you calling her name, and if she's very focused she may even forget to eat or go to the bathroom for hours. It is easy for her to concentrate on the puzzle because she really enjoys it, and is good at it. Other examples of common flow states include things like exercising, playing games, writing code, playing a musical instrument, or gardening. Anything that requires some skill to do.

It's this last feature, skill, which is the critical factor in a flow experience. Across the board, people in a flow state describe the pleasure that comes from mastering a series of small challenges over and over. Flow does involve work, but it is work that you like doing and can do well. If a challenge is too difficult, frustration and disappointment arise, and that blocks the flow state. Flow has to involve a task you can actually achieve. On the other hand, if the task is too easy, it doesn't capture your attention, and flow cannot happen either. You get bored and float away into distraction. In between anxiety when the task is too hard, and boredom when it's too easy, there is a Goldilocks zone for the flow state; a condition of a task that is *just right*. If you're involved in doing something that falls into your Goldilocks zone, what we might call the "flow channel," then flow can take place. The secret, then, to good concentration (according to Csikszentmihalyi) is to learn how to make any task you are doing just the right level of difficulty for you.

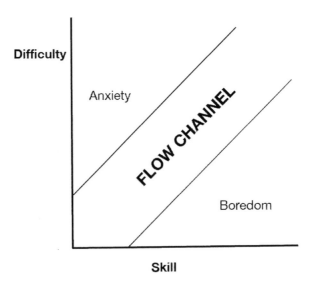

In his research Csikszentmihalyi found that people felt that their experiences of flow were some of the most cherished, valuable, and pleasurable activities in their lives. They describe it in glowing terms like "ecstatic" and "floating" and "effortless." Here's a quote I found from a computer coder:

"The experience of programming in the zone for me was tremendously satisfying, relaxing and (I believe) hyper-productive. It was not an everyday experience. It could not be planned or scheduled. I could not force myself into the state."[98]

Sounds good. But there is a curious feature in most of Csikszentmihalyi's many quotes from people who enjoy flow. Quite often they say that "it just happens" and that there's "nothing they can do" to get themselves into that state, as in the quote above. Their strategies to get into the zone mainly involve just doing their activity every day, hoping that today is a good day for achieving flow. Sometimes it happens, sometimes is doesn't. It's hit or miss.

But does it really have to be that way? Couldn't there be a way to induce flow so that it's not just a happy accident? Csikszentmihalyi's formula for achieving flow involves manipulating the *difficulty* of the activity in order to induce it. You adjust the level of difficulty to match your skill level until you hit the Goldilocks zone. But there is another possibility that I don't believe Csikszentmihalyi ever mentions: cultivating your *ability to focus*. Intentionally training your concentration ability so that it's much stronger than normal. And, as you might have guessed by now, I'm here to tell you that meditation is a powerful and effective way to do just that. A host of studies have shown that one of the chief measurable effects of meditation training is to increase your attention levels.[99]

One major study looked at people in a intensive meditation retreat, who were meditating ten to twelve hours a day for three full months.[100] That's a major commitment of time and energy, but it gives us a rare chance to look at what meditation can achieve at the extreme end of the scale. The study used a phenomenon known as "attentional blink" to measure the subject's ability to pay attention. Let's say you flash a series of letters on a screen very quickly. Embedded in the series are two numbers. If the numbers are far enough apart in time, you will notice both. But if the numbers get close enough together in time, less than half a second apart, then subjects notice the first number, but miss the second one. There is a kind of "blink" in attention, a moment when your awareness is not involved in what you are doing.

There are many theories as to why the attentional blink happens, but it was thought to be a fixed property of the human brain. The meditators proved this wrong, however. After three months of intensive training, the attentional blink had all but disappeared—they could detect both numbers in the sequence even when presented at high speed. Meditation had enhanced their concentration skill to a degree thought previously impossible. Of course, most people don't have a spare three months to spend meditating twelve hours a day, but even a few days of meditation training significantly improves your concentration.[101]

I majored in languages at university, primarily German. Language instruction at the undergraduate level mainly consists of reading literature in that language—it's even called a "German literature" degree. We not only read fiction authors like Kafka, Brecht, and Goethe, but quite a selection of nonfiction: Kant, Nietzsche, Marx, and so on. I read most of these avidly, soaking up the cultural education as much as the linguistic. Yet after college I went to Japan, and from there all over the world, and didn't do much with my German language skills for almost thirty years.

When I was studying psychology, however, I found the need to go a bit deeper with certain source authors, such as Freud and Jung. Jung's classic *Memories, Dreams, Reflections* had always been high on my someday-reading list, so I started there. But in a nod to my collegiate self, I decided to buy the book in German, rather than English, and prepared to grind my way through it. Having barely touched a German language book in three decades, I knew it would be a long haul. But what happened next really surprised me.

I didn't have that hard a time reading it. At first I thought it must be that Jung was a gifted author, and I figured it might be that it was a particularly engrossing text. Still, that couldn't quite explain what was happening. I needed a dictionary, of course, and spent time puzzling over certain idiomatic phrases I had never seen before. But it just wasn't the brutal slog I had been expecting. Instead, I felt enjoyably absorbed in the reading, taking notes, looking things up, and pondering the ideas. I was in a nice flow state reading something that should have been kind of hard for me.

As I cast my mind back over the years to my college days, I knew that reading any serious, adult-level, nonfiction German book had never been this effortless in college. The fact that it was easy now just didn't seem to make sense. Language skills degrade over time; they get worse, not better. And yet here I was smoothly flowing through this complex text with ease and even enjoyment. What was going on?

Then I remembered the salient point: in the intervening thirty years I had done intensive meditation training—i.e. three decades of hard-core concentration practice. And that's when it clicked. I actually wasn't any better at reading German. In fact, my skills in that language had probably degraded right on schedule for someone my age. I had been pretty good in university, so now my abilities were adequate. But what had radically improved since college was *my ability to concentrate*. To apply my mind continuously and totally to a problem.

That is an example of how meditation can expand the Goldilocks zone for achieving a flow state. Because meditation functions as training in concentration, it gets harder and harder to get either bored or anxious. Remember that the formula for concentration is simply to bring your attention back to a focus object repeatedly. That is both the essence and the totality of concentration practice. Having iterated through this in meditation for a while, you can focus pleasurably on things you would've otherwise found really boring, and also on things that are hard enough to have put you off before.

It's one of the secrets to making meditation work for you in life: make the effort to meditate on things that are just slightly too hard for your focus ability. This stretches your capacity to handle the anxiety of a task that's a little hard. Alternately, you can sometimes go back to meditating on something you find intrinsically boring. By maintaining curiosity and interest with a boring focus object, you will discover that it begins to become strangely interesting. As the founder of the Mindfulness Based Stress Reduction program popular in US hospitals, Jon Kabat Zinn, says, "When you pay attention to boredom, it gets unbelievably interesting."

Paying close attention even when you feel bored expands your flow channel, making it wider until it becomes quite easy to get into a flow state. You will find yourself in a mild flow state most of the time, and could find yourself in a pretty deep one when you're meditating. By adjusting your concentration in this way to achieve this state, everything you do all day can become more fun, interesting, and fulfilling. This is especially true in meditation, which, by building concentration, can help you find flow in your life.

CHAPTER NINETEEN

Distraction-free Living

Concentration is the opposite of distraction. We tend to think that concentration is a difficult thing to do, but most people don't have a strong opinion about distractions. That gives you an opportunity to make a clever hack: you can remove distractions as the first step to developing better concentration. You probably won't have as much resistance to it, and eliminating some distractions from your life, will make building your concentration much easier.

If something is pulling your attention away from your chosen concentration object, that is distraction. Distraction dilutes brainpower, frazzles the nerves, and results in non-optimum outcomes. You end up stressed out and spun around, and don't even get the satisfaction of a job well done. We supposedly live in a multitasking world, but multitasking (called "task switching" in neuroscience) is very inefficient, mainly because there is a cognitive cost each time you switch between tasks.[102]

The cure is to do one thing at a time. That's it in a nutshell. Do just what you're doing and don't do anything else. It's that *else* that causes so much trouble. Here are five types of distraction-causing things that you can easily remove in order to get more focused:

Shut off all other input — Binge-watching *Silicon Valley* episodes while doing your taxes might not be such a good idea. Shut off everything that is not related to what you're doing. No music, no videos, no movies, no Internet, no texting. Unless you need it for work (or whatever it is you're doing), turn it off until you are ready to give it 100 percent of your attention. Having media on in the background actually uses up a large portion of the neurons that could otherwise be employed on the task at hand. Think: one thing at a time.

If you need to use the Internet, block out all other web activities — Do not check Twitter or Facebook—close those tabs—and shut off any alerts, badges, or other ways apps have of grabbing your attention. Do not click on any links or bookmarks that do not take you directly to a site relevant to the task you are doing. Many writing programs now include a full screen mode that blocks out all other windows, which is really helpful to create focus.

Filter your email — You may have to use email for work, but you don't have to be subjected to every notification you get from a social networking site or forwarded joke from your great aunt. They are not urgent, and these interruptions each use up a little bit of brainpower. While you're working, keep personal emails to a bare minimum. Better yet, get separate accounts for work and personal emails so that you can work without interruption. This will be good for your personal time, too, since work emails will not intrude.

Tame your phone — The smartphone is there to serve you, not the other way around. Unless you really need to be contacted, keep it off or at least silent. Stop checking it and most importantly switch off as many notices, badges, and alerts as you possibly can. Do not even look at it except to make a necessary call, or to check work email. If you can leave it turned off in another room while you get some work done, or focus on a quiet evening with your significant other, all the better. Decide what your phone is actually *for*, and use it only for that purpose.

Keep non-essential talk to a minimum — When you are trying to focus on a task, gabbing with others is just another form of irrelevant throughput. Cooperatively working toward a common goal with people we like is one of life's most satisfying activities, but listening to a coworker dump about their bad date isn't helping you finish your next task. Without being rude, just keep moving things toward silent, efficient completion. If, on the other hand, it is time to talk with your coworker, give speaking and listening your full attention. Of course, try to do this without being uptight or controlling. There are polite ways to let people know that you are busy.

Remember that these tips don't just count for work. If you're playing a game, play the game. If you're making love, make love. If you're walking in nature, just walk and enjoy.

These are just a few of the basics, but you get the idea. There are many ways to adapt these to suit your own life circumstance. Pulling the plug on all these distractions can be disconcerting at first. You may feel disoriented, anxious, or alone. Many of us have a gnarly dopamine addiction, and can't bear not to check our phone constantly. So take it easy and undo distraction at your own pace. Once you get a taste for a more concentrated experience, it will take on a life of its own. Being present and concentrated feels good, and is immensely more fulfilling.

Crank Machines

Mammals are wired to look for novelty in the environment, a behavior called "seeking." In his research, neuroscientist and psychologist Jaak Panksepp discovered an interesting feature of the networks in mammalian brains, particularly rats. If you place an electrode in the area for sexual stimulation, for example, and provide the rat with a button that will stimulate the electrode, the rat will press it for a while, achieve satisfaction, and then stop pressing the button, until another day. He or she is now satisfied, and doesn't look for further sexual stimulation. The same thing happens with hunger and sleep. The rat will press the button until satisfied, become euphoric and relaxed, and then rest, or do something else.

If, however, you place the electrode in the area that stimulates seeking behavior (the lateral hypothalamus), you'll witness something very different. The rat will press the button, and press the button, and press the button, and never reach satisfaction. Rather than becoming euphoric and relaxed, the rat will become crazed, strung out, frenzied; pushing the button until it collapses. They've done experiments a bit like this on humans, too, with similar results. The neuroscience behind this is fascinating, but the short version is this: your brain is wired to seek, and it gets a dopamine hit each time it does.[103] Dopamine is the same neurotransmitter stimulated by drugs like cocaine and methamphetamine. It makes you feel focused, energized, and good at first, but after a while you just feel stressed, sketchy, and burnt out.

The trouble is that evolution did not favor animals that sat around all fat, happy, and satisfied with themselves. While they may have been the happiest creatures ever to live, they were also probably the first to become dinner for other, less satisfied seekers. Or they perished because they didn't spend enough time looking for new opportunities in their surroundings. This means that the system in your brain is rigged: there seems to be much more drive to seek than to be rewarded. We would rather look than actually find.

The seeking urge is deeply baked into the brains of mammals, and it is deeply baked into you. It evolved to help you to thrive in a prehistoric world in which novelty was a rarity, a strange and wonderful newness in an enormous ocean of relative stability and predictability. The world of boring sameness is the world our brain expects, and it's why we get so addicted to the new, the exciting, and the strange. Our ancestors needed sugar and so we are saddled with a sweet tooth that is killing us, because we now live in a sugar-saturated world. In the same way, our ancestors evolved in a world where almost nothing interesting ever happened, and so we are stuck with a real hankering for anything new. The rub is that we now exist in an environment with an endless supply of intense novel stimuli. If television is a fire hose of raw emotional intensity and mental novelty delivered into your living room, the Internet is a tsunami. Our brains have an insatiable urge for seeking new things, but now we have a limitless source of novelty. We are stuffed beyond the limit with unprocessed, undigested, and unhelpful experiences that we cannot convert to energizing, useful, practical knowledge. We can't stop pressing the seek button, looking for another hit of dopamine. We are information junkies, and our brains are full. Like rats in a lab, we could just keep hitting the seek button until we collapse. The effect is even stronger if the seeking contains an element of randomness.[104]

To a human brain, a smartphone loaded with flashy lights, "random" notifications, addictive games, music, videos, shopping, and porn, as well as instant access to the latest news and information, makes a device that is almost irresistible. We are powerfully motivated to check texts, emails, and other message channels over and over, because there just *might* be something cool or interesting there. If we don't check it, there is a fear that we might miss out on an opportunity (a date, a job, a cool concert) or not hear about a threat (a traffic jam, a market dip, a problem with a loved one). It's not that those happen that often, but something interesting enough happens often enough that we just have to keep checking, seeking that never-ending dopamine hit.

It would be best if you could turn off your smartphone completely while trying to meditate, but practically there are certain calls that it wouldn't be safe or responsible to miss. Sometimes turning it all the way off actually increases anxiety to the point where it's worse for concentration. Yet leaving the phone all the way on while you're trying to sit mindfully constitutes the Death Star of distraction.

Luckily, there is an answer: smartphones come with a "Do Not Disturb" mode, which allows you to silence all but the most important interruptions. In the preferences settings, you can set the phone to allow only calls from, say, your teenager, and silence all other interruptions. You can set it exactly to whatever makes it easiest for you to relax and focus while still feeling comfortable. If you want to go for broke, just completely disable email and web browsing during the day, or whenever you're trying to focus.

Full screen Mode — Most of the interruptions and distractions present on the phone are also present on our desktop computers, probably even more so. In response to plummeting productivity, and the near helplessness we may feel around keeping focused in the face of this distraction deluge, many popular applications have added a "full screen mode," as I mentioned above. This means that while you work with this application it blacks out all other applications. A simple but useful feature that instantly removes major sources of distraction.

Another fast-growing genre of applications cuts off the Internet from all your devices. Here is a current list of applications for your computer that will help cut down distractions. (You can help me keep it updated in the future—these things change fast.)

> **AwayFind** awayfind.com
> **Buddhify** buddhify.com
> **Calm Down** mermodynamics.com/calmdown/
> **Calm Your Box** calmbox.me
> **Flux** stereopsis.com/flux
> **HeartMath** heartmath.com
> **Mac Freedom** macfreedom.com
> **OmmWriter** ommwriter.com
> **ReWire** rewireapp.com
> **Shroud** sabi.net/nriley/software/

Getting rid of badges and notifications — We are also an extremely social species that evolved to prioritize friends and family above all else. One of the catchiest aspects of a smartphone is its ability to notify you of incoming items of interest. Text messages, calendar alerts, Facebook updates, emails, retweets and follows—there's a seemingly endless stream of things you could possibly want to be alerted about, and the smartphone caters to all of them. If you are a doctor or fire fighter, getting such alerts makes a lot of sense: your job requires it. For the rest of us, getting alerted all the time is just another way to get constantly interrupted.

White noise — If you're in an environment that is noisy, the best thing to do is to get rid of as much of the noise as possible. However, there are many situations where that's not possible or practical. Even so, there is still something you can do to counteract the negative effects all that random noise has on your concentration—use white noise. White noise means sound that is many frequencies at once, without any particular signal or information. It sounds like static, or the hissing of a radio tuned to no station.

In one sense it is pure noise pollution, but there is a way that it can really help you. White noise, it turns out, is perfect to drowning out other noises. For example, if there are a lot of cars, beeping, voices, ambulances, and so on in your environment all the time, these sounds are very distracting because they are something specific to pay attention to. If you have white noise playing in your space loud enough, however, it will cover up these distracting sounds. And because white noise has nothing in it to pay attention to—your brain interprets it as environmental background sound, like wind in the trees—it allows you to overcome the distraction these other sounds would have caused.

This fight-fire-with-fire strategy has been proven to be effective in many experiments. There are a lot of white noise makers for sale on the market, but you don't have to buy one to get some white noise for yourself. For example, here is a link to 12 solid hours of white noise, totally free, which you can play in the background to help you concentrate.[105]

For Cthulhu's Sake, Just Turn It Off

Many of us have to use the Internet for work, and our smartphones may be vital links to our family, children, and others. Tricks like the ones above can be lifesavers in terms of making the flood of information and alerts something we can cope with in a sustainable way. However, there are many times when these devices just aren't necessary at all. How many times do you find yourself checking your email in bed, or compulsively texting when you're out for dinner with a friend? Situations like these represent a *voluntary* immersion in the digital deluge. And that is a whole lot of distraction that you have complete power over. All you have to do is turn it off.

It's crucial to remember that your attention is one of the most precious capacities you possess. In an environment where individuals have the equivalent of what would previously have been newspapers (blogging), radio stations (podcasting) and television networks (YouTube), we are bombarded with far too many things to pay attention to. We are forced to choose between virtually unlimited places to focus our attention. Each of these sources is involved in an epic Darwinian-capitalistic struggle to grab our eyeballs and therefore our cash. They don't call it the "attention economy" for nothing.

Surrounded by such a wealth of interestingness, each person has the opportunity to become a connoisseur. We have the chance to redefine and rebuild our relationship to our own attention networks in the brain. Instead of working hard to find something interesting to pay attention to, and being surprised and delighted when it manifests, we now are being called upon to create much higher standards for what we'll pay attention to. We have to decide what is worth noticing, and what sorts of subjects we want to give our full attention. After that we have to practice ruthlessly discarding anything that doesn't meet our higher standards.

This is a new situation for most human beings, one that is very different than the environment in which we evolved. It will take conscious effort, real clarity about our goals, and a much more active stance with regard to the world around us. Yet it will be more than worth it.

Decide how much time per day you actually need to interact with the virtual world and stick to that amount. After that, turn it off and do something embodied and in the real world. Remember the world outside the screen? Filled with people and animals and plants and sky and stuff? Why not check that out for a while? Time away from overwhelming technology is really restorative. Giving your seeking system a break feels remarkably good, and you might even find yourself in a flow state. So turn off the screens for a while, and take a nice deep breath of the real world.

CHAPTER TWENTY

Learning to Listen

You had a bad time with your partner yesterday, and today you're having intense emotions about it. You feel upset and confused, there's so much going on. You meet your friend at a coffee shop, hoping to talk it out. But as soon as you start, she starts rubbing and poking the screen of her smartphone. As you start telling her the details of your relationship problems, she says, "Uh-huh, uh-huh." Heart sinking, you soldier on, and eventually she puts the device away and actually makes eye contact. That's almost worse. Watching her eyes, you can see her flipping through a database of automatic responses as you speak. "You have to stand up for yourself," she interjects, sipping foam off her latte. It's a stock line that makes you wonder if anyone, anywhere is capable of just listening. It might be time to pay for a therapy session, just to get some quality attention.

Listening effectively is a powerful skill, yet few people in our society have taken the time to develop it. Most people will talk more or less continuously, and when they actually are quiet, they are thinking of what they are going to say next while pretending to listen to others. "Conversation" becomes a duel of clever sound bites, delivered with little interest in what others are saying. How often do you have some remark locked and loaded, ready to fire, just waiting for a pause in the other person's remarks? If there's a moment of silence, we nervously jump in, filling it with speech.

If you listen for a few minutes to two people talking like this, you will notice several features about the conversation. First, there is never any silence. Second, because there is no silence, the conversationalists are never actually *taking in* what the other person is saying. They are not actually listening. Third, since they aren't taking it in, they aren't really thinking about it or responding to what's being said in a meaningful way. The conversation skates along on the shallowest possible level, a mere tennis match of rote verbal reactions triggering rote verbal reactions. Conversations like this are extremely tiring. They contain no food for the brain or heart; the verbal equivalent of junk food—empty, unsatisfying, and ultimately bad for you. And given the shortness of life, why even bother?

Learning to listen means learning to actually pay attention to—to concentrate on—what other people are saying. To really listen, you use your concentration skills on the sounds of speech entering your ears. You listen to your conversation partner's words as if listening to a favorite song, with your mind focused on what they are saying and what it means. This kind of concentrated listening is also called "active listening" or "deep listening." Deep listening is an excellent concentration practice in and of itself. Beyond that, it gives enjoyment of music, other humans, and most importantly it brings a profound, positive shift in the quality of your relationships.

Listening with concentration can be called active listening because you are not just passively allowing speech to enter your ears. Instead, you bring as much of your listening capacity into the act as possible. Like some kind of highly concentrated alien life form, your ears become hungry for the words they are listening to, and chew the words as finely as possible before digesting them.

The first step in learning to listen is to learn to be *quiet*. Make a friend of silence. This can be difficult because nobody wants to be judged as being dull. There is a natural desire to respond quickly, and to be seen as interesting and smart. But if you resist this urge even a little bit, it removes the reactivity from conversation, and opens up the space for some actual responding.

Try this experiment: When talking with someone, play a mental game of waiting *one full second* before responding to anything they have said. That's it, just one second of silence, no matter what you're talking about. This is a long, long time in a normal conversation. During this second of silence, it may seem like enough time for the pyramids to get built. Don't think about what you are going to say, think about what the other person has just said. Give it one long, delicious second of your full concentrated, attention. Then respond, saying whatever it is you have to say. Make sure to maintain eye contact so that they know you're listening to what they're saying and considering it.

You will be surprised what a big difference this little game makes. By actually giving the other person's words a moment to sink in before you respond, your connection with that person, the depth of your conversation, will be very noticeable. Because humans love to be heard, the speaker will begin to say things and respond in ways that are very positive. But the biggest changes will be in you. The practice derails the reactivity in your conversation. You will feel yourself opening to the person in a new way. Even if you strongly dislike their ideas, you will begin to open to the person emotionally, and feel into their humanness. They will feel it, too. It's a powerful feeling, one that immediately begins to relieve our chronic condition of existential isolation.

As you learn to do this, try to listen even more deeply while the other person is speaking. Dedicate the entire time they are speaking to actually hearing and considering their words, not listening to your own mental reaction to them. If you practice this enough, you will have some of the best conversations you've ever had. People will remark at how kind and empathic you seem. And they will begin to slow down and listen to you as well.

Want to connect with people? Want to really understand where people are at and what's going on? Let some silence happen and make a practice of deep listening.

CHAPTER TWENTY ONE

Sensory Clarity

When I was a teenager, we got cable TV, which was a brand new thing back then. There were few programs available and even fewer movies. I watched (the original) *Space 1999* all the time, and saw the (original) movies *Rollerball* and Polanski's *The Tenant* dozens of times each. That was almost all there was to watch. This repetition felt like a metaphor for my life then. The boredom seemed crushing and almost painful. New people reminded me of people whom I already knew. Life felt like a rerun of the same stale old patterns, and nothing was interesting or new, and I would do almost anything to find a new experience that was exciting and fresh. This sometimes led me to unwise behaviors in an attempt to jazz things up a bit.

The Greek philosopher Heraclitus said that you couldn't step in the same river twice. He meant, of course, that nothing is *actually* ever the same. Science agrees: the arrow of time is moving in a single direction, and every moment is completely fresh and new. The world, the whole universe, never repeats itself. There is no possibility for repetition, so why is it that it often doesn't feel that way?

The answer is simple: it's not the world that is boring and repetitive, it's your mind that is boring and repetitive. Your thoughts can sound like a broken record. When I first started meditating on my thinking (a somewhat advanced mindfulness practice), I noticed this fact right away. Sometimes new ideas would pop up, but most of the time it's just grinding over the same old territory. We mostly go through life unaware of this, but even a few minutes of concentrated observation of your mental activity will demonstrate how stale your thinking really is. For every new, creative, interesting thought that enters your head, there are a thousand thoughts like, "I never should have bought that damn car," repeating over and over.

Our experience wasn't always like this. When we were children, we saw things directly, and that is one of the main reasons why we remember childhood as so magical. Education is an excellent thing, but in our society we educate people into a mental/conceptual relationship with life and away from an experiential relationship with it. A conceptual outlook is a useful tool that allows you to plan a vacation, balance your checkbook, and read a fascinating book. We could never get along without it. But in the modern world, it has gotten a bit overactive and is running all the time, even when it's not required for problem solving. Instead, we've gotten stuck in our minds, unable to let go of our driven, conceptual thinking when we want to. It's one thing to have a useful tool, and quite another to be chained to the tool, unable to let go of it when you don't need it.

When was the last time you actually encountered a tree as a tree? It's possible to see a tree as a sensory phenomenon: the rich texture and scent of the bark, the luscious colors of the leaves, the sound it makes as the wind passes through it, and so on. This is the sensory experience of a tree. Yet most of us pass dozens or hundreds of trees a day, and we notice none of these features. We barely encounter trees as sensory experiences at all. Instead, we simply reduce all this sensory richness into a single word, "tree," and leave it at that. The word tree functions as a concept, or symbol—mental shorthand that allows us to shortcut having to actually encounter the tree.

This mental shortcut is a big advantage in terms of functioning in the world. It's a very efficient way to process information. Imagine if on the way to work, you had to stop and have a deep, rich, sensory experience with everything you passed on the way. You'd never arrive. You'd be too busy rolling around with a dog on the grass, or staring at the clouds, or listening to music you heard coming out of a shop. You'd get fired, or flunk out of school, or lose your relationship. The brain only has so much processing power. So it's an integral part of our life as adults to be able to focus on what we deem to be important, and what's important in our society is *concepts*.

But there is a major downside to all this efficiency, of course. The downside is that when work is done, and you want to have some fun, you have a hard time. You want to listen to some amazing music, or make love with your partner, or really enjoy a walk in the woods, but you can't get out of your head. You're stuck in a rut of mental talk talk talk. You've gotten too habituated to seeing things as concepts, rather than as sensory experiences. Your mind has become metaphorically like a video game in which trees, people, art, and the beauty of the world have been reduced to a functional, blocky, low-resolution screen. Not very enjoyable. You've lost the connection to your senses; to what poet Mary Oliver calls "the soft animal of your body."

We evolved from animals, and we require a connection to our senses in order to feel safe, comfortable, happy, and joyous. This is what people are talking about when they talk about "embodiment." Embodiment means being in touch with the lush world of the senses. The colors of light. The nuances of sound. The textures of touch. This is where connection to the world, the present moment, and the body exist. People use booze or other sedatives to knock their endless conceptual blather offline and get into their body, but this is a brute-force method with a lot of drawbacks, like hangovers and addiction. Plus it partially defeats itself, since it tends to be numbing to be the body, too. Drink may get you back in your senses, but your senses will be foggy and fuzzy.

We of the geeky persuasion are particularly susceptible to getting trapped in the conceptual mind. Part of having a strong mental apparatus is being able to parse, juggle, and remix concepts with relative ease. Being good at something is enjoyable, and so we play in the mental realm more than most. On top of that, society rewards people for being smart by paying them a lot of money, which has big benefits like physical safety, health insurance, greater amounts of free time, higher levels of social status, and so on. So we also become heavily conditioned to stay up in our heads.

Given all this, I think we have an even more pressing need to take a break from the mental realm and get in touch with our bodies. The trouble is that climbing out of your head can feel like you're giving up your greatest asset—your intelligence—and embracing something that you're actually not very good at. The body is for cavemen, not the astronauts, it's for people who can dance. The best we do, usually, is fueling ourselves with the artisanal cocktails (perhaps brewing and distilling it ourselves) and finding some mental downtime that way. Or playing video games. That's relaxing, right? There's nothing wrong with any of that, except that in my opinion, we need to learn more effective ways to get out of the head and into the body. That way, we can do it anytime and anywhere we want to. At lunch at work. In the car. During a five-minute walk. Times and places when substances or distractions may not work.

One of the major benefits of mindfulness meditation is that it teaches you to rediscover your senses in a healthy and clear way. After a long day at work, you can use mindfulness meditation to voluntarily let go of your fixated, driven mental world. You can, at will, see the deep beauty in your lover's eyes. The colors of the forest. The satisfaction of simple foods. Even the basic pleasure of having a nice bed with clean sheets to sleep in. Such experiences are not sentimental remembrances, but immediate, sensory events. Experiencing them only requires re-learning how to contact the senses directly, without (or at least bypassing somewhat) the mediation of the conceptual mind. There are lots of ways to help this process along. Taking an art class, playing music, writing poetry, cooking meals—any similar epicurean activities that focus on the enjoyment of the senses will begin to re-ignite your passion for the non-conceptual part of life. Because it concentrates directly on learning how to contact the senses themselves, rather than relying on some particular, external thing like food or music, mindfulness meditation is probably the most powerful way to do this.

The fact is that the rainbows and unicorns world of childhood never went away, you just got trained to think that beauty is unimportant and frivolous. It's waiting for you, on the other side of your mental world of concepts, judgments, fantasies, and preoccupations. When the poet William Blake wrote:

> *To see the world in a grain of sand,*
> *And a heaven in a wild flower,*
> *Hold infinity in the palm of your hand,*
> *And eternity in an hour.*

he was talking about the direct experience of the senses. The renovating power of the world is possible with even a small amount of mindfulness practice. Then, after a long day at work, you can let go of thinking, enjoy a tasty meal, play with your child, even just take a bath, and deeply enjoy it. *Geeks of the world, unite! You have nothing to lose but your conceptual chains.*[106]

More Life

In a way, our experience of life is nothing but the experience of our senses. Without our sensory contact with others, the world, and ourselves we would be on the level of fungus or bacteria—existing, but without any experience of existing.[107] Of course, conscious awareness is the key to knowing we exist, but what is it that we are consciously aware of 99.99999... percent of the time? Sensory experience. This is especially true if we include thinking and imagination as "internal senses," as internal analogs of seeing and hearing.

If our experience life is nothing but a sensory experience, then what does it mean to actually increase our sensory clarity? You'd think that enhancing the resolution on the central sense of aliveness would revolutionize your life, and you'd be right. It opens the door to an absolutely profound change in the depth of enjoyment and meaning we derive from existence. You could almost say in a metaphoric sense that increased sensory clarity gives you more life, since each moment of life can be experienced at a "higher resolution."

Working with sensory clarity is the main way, in my opinion, to boost the development of your insula. This is speculation, but given that the insula is concerned with feeling sensations in the body, the more you focus on the minute details of those sensations, it is probable that you are building connectivity in the insula. And remember that the insula is extremely important in understanding how you are feeling, as well as connecting with other people. The way I see it, reaching toward more sensory clarity builds the insula, and growing the insula enhances sensory clarity. This creates a powerful feedback loop, and is a great example of using brain plasticity in your favor.

While the above only applies to body sensation, concentrating on gaining sensory clarity in the other senses probably does something similar in those domains. You are cultivating your ability to connect deeply, completely, and in many different ways to the present moment. As I've mentioned, curiosity is one of the main ways to cultivate concentration. Combine this with openness and nonjudgment, and you've got a recipe for growing sensory clarity. You'll find yourself drawn in more and more deeply to the details of things. It's unavoidable.

The world of the senses is the world of the present moment. It's an embodied realm, outside the slick-but-shallow virtual world of the conceptual mind. Contacting your senses automatically begins to pull you out of your mental preoccupations and into what is happening right here and now. As we'll see in a later chapter, there are a lot of advantages to that, including real-word enhancements of physical and mental wellbeing. One of the big benefits is that you don't miss out on your own life. It's all too easy to be lost in the clouds while exquisite things are occurring right at your feet. We spend money on expensive food but are distracted at dinner and don't taste it. We buy beautiful objects but are quickly bored and ignore them. Under those conditions, what's the point of acquiring such things in the first place? Why take a vacation if you can't stop thinking about work concerns on the beach in paradise? Intentionally cultivating sensory clarity in meditation will help you with all of these issues. The senses are like an anchor into the present moment, and that is were all the action is. That's where your life is.

Stuck in a Good Place

As a meditation teacher, I often run into people who present me with the following problem: They have been meditating for a long time, usually between five and fifteen years. When they first started practicing, they made a lot of progress and had big insights. It changed their life, and they got a lot of benefit out of it. The practice is helping them to be nicer to other people, to experience less anxiety, and to be more focused at work. But for several years now, their practice has plateaued. They're dedicated and they enjoy their practice, but don't feel that they're still making progress or getting new insights.

This situation is called "getting stuck in a good place." They've gotten to a certain depth in their practice, but they don't know how to go any deeper. If the idea is to make the unconscious conscious, they've excavated down to a certain level, but don't know how to dig any further. At least 95 percent of the time the answer is very simple: they need to learn to cultivate greater sensory clarity. Exploring smaller and subtler dimensions of sensation is the key to getting out of this rut.

Let me explain. Typically the initial instructions beginning meditators are given is to "meditate on body sensations." They are told to look at a few interesting aspects of these sensations. And that short instruction gets them all the benefit that I'm calling the "good place." But the reason they've become stuck is because the instructions can only take them so far. It's like their meditation engine has run out of fuel. The growth in brain structure it took to get them to this point has worked its magic. But now they have adapted to this level of contact with sensation, and aren't pushing to go any further. So the secret is to begin investigating more and more minute levels of detail in sensation. To increase the resolution of your senses, so to speak.

In the realm of the body, this means to get even more curious about the fine details of body sensations. There are several ways to work on cultivating this. For one, I've often noticed that people tend to think of body sensations as being flat, two-dimensional. But, since the body is a *three-dimensional* object, body sensations are not typically flat, but instead are 3D. That means they can have a very complex morphology, which is interesting to explore. They can take various shapes: spherical, cubic, star-shaped, conic, cylindrical, etc. Of course, real sensations are almost never perfect geometric solids, but you can guess which one a particular sensation is closest to. Three-dimensional sensations can have "sides." The top can feel different from the bottom. The front can feel different from the back, and so on. Dimensionality also means that they not only have a surface area, but a *volume*, and those different areas within that volume can feel quite different. For example, a sensation might have a rather neutral, mushy quality making up the bulk of its mass. But floating within that mass of oatmeal, there might be "raisins," so to speak. Little spots of intense, pointy sensations. So this three-dimensionality of body sensation opens up a vastly more complex and detailed possibility for exploration. And the same goes for emotional sensations.

Another aspect of body sensation that can increase your sensory clarity is the fact that it isn't always solid or stable. Many sensations feel as if they are the same, moment to moment. They don't seem to be changing or moving very much at all. But certain sensations are not so steady. They can be getting stronger or weaker, larger or smaller. They can move around, from location to location, or alter their shape and 3D morphology. So as you're meditating on a sensation, notice if it, or any little part of it, is changing in any way. Maybe just the corner is throbbing or pulsing. Maybe it's slightly shifting its center back and forth a few millimeters. Maybe one side of it is swelling out a bit and then deflating back. To quote the floating head of Carl Sagan in a jar, there are "billions and billions" of possibilities.

A third way to increase sensory clarity is to investigate areas of the body that you don't normally investigate. If you were to keep a list of body regions that you have contacted in meditation, you would discover that there are some spots that for whatever reason you never contact. How about the upper palate of your mouth? The back of your ear? The inside line of the spine? Inside your joints? Take the path less traveled. Seek out and find the out of the way places that you have never previously meditated upon, and bring them online. As well as helping to clarify sensation, this can have a surprisingly powerful effect on your sense of integration.

A fourth method for going deeper into sensation is to act like a microscope. Get curious and look at sensations on as fine a scale as you can. If you're used to golf ball-sized sensation units, try feeling marble-sized ones. If you marble-sized sensations are easy for you to contact, see if you can begin feeling into sensations that are pea-sized. What about sensations the size of a grain of sand? Learning to sense these smaller and smaller sensations will really boost your sensory clarity. You really cannot overdo this way of working.

A variation on this is attempting to feel more and more subtle sensations. It's possible to get stuck only feeling sensations that are intense or "loud." So get curious about contacting sensations that are very subtle or "light."

There is a fifth method that works in a very different way to boost sensory clarity. Rather than upping the resolution, it works by making fine distinctions between *types* of sensations. For example, you can distinguish between pleasant and unpleasant sensations, two very basic categories that provide a lot of insight into your experience. But

178

it's possible to get nerdier than that. Try distinguishing between "textures" of sensation: smooth, rough, sharp, mushy, bumpy, goopy, tingly, stinging, and so on. Or note the difference between sensations that are moving and those that are still. Subcategorize those into sensations that are moving left-right, up-down, forward-backward, or in other directions. Distinguish wave-like movement from broken movement. And so on.

I remember once spending an entire weeklong meditation retreat meditating on tiny, subtle sensations in my skeletal structure. Even though I'd been hearing about the power of sensory clarity from Shinzen for a long time, that was the point where I realized how amazing it really is. Cultivating sensory clarity in all the senses has enriched my meditation practice far beyond anything I could have imagined. And, of course, it's led to positive life changes, and a real sense of wellbeing that I can't help but want to offer to you. Take the time to get deeply, deeply into your own sensory experience, and discover the place where you are really alive as if for the first time.

CHAPTER TWENTY TWO

Building Resilience

There is a pivotal moment in *Dune* when Paul Atreides (later known as "Muad'dib") and his mother Jessica must flee or die. Having been betrayed by the family doctor, Paul's father Duke Leto is dead, their army is destroyed, their house broken, and everything is in ruins. Escaping in an ornithopter, they head for the only available sanctuary: the open desert. After crash landing their aircraft, Paul and Jessica immediately have to run for their lives from a giant sandworm that eats their ornithopter. They survive, but now they're stuck all alone in a harsh, difficult desert filled with deadly animals, terrible storms, and building-size worms tunneling beneath them. Raised on a different planet, they have little idea how to deal with the environment. They face a long journey into the unknown, with tragedy behind them and almost certain death before them.

At this desperate juncture, Paul calmly states, "I find myself enjoying the quiet here." His mother, a trained in the ways of the Bene Gesserit witches, recalls one of the sisterhood's axioms, *"The mind can go either direction under stress—toward positive or toward negative: on or off. Think of it as a spectrum whose extremes are unconsciousness at the negative end and hyperconsciousness at the positive end. The way the mind will lean under stress is strongly influenced by training."*[108]

Paul's composure in this harrowing circumstance is really surprising. Most people would've been shattered by grief or overwhelmed by the tasks ahead. It's the kind of situation that would test anyone's mettle, as they say. The fact that Paul can relax and enjoy the scenery is probably due to the fact that mom has shared her Bene Gesserit teachings with him throughout his childhood. She taught him to react positively to new challenges under stress, and his training pays off in this case with what will become literally epic results.

Responding gracefully under stress is a hallmark of wellbeing. It epitomizes the quality known as resilience, which is the ability to bounce back in the face of adversity. How long would it take you to get over a major breakup? The death of a loved one? A sandworm attack? Would you spend months at home in bed with the curtains drawn or would you be able to function, despite the overwhelming emotions, thoughts, and experiences? For too many people, a big emotional setback can push them to the brink of dysfunction; to the place where they may mismanage their life, take up destructive behaviors or addictions, lose their job, or make other poor decisions. These are not indicative of character flaws, but are the direct result of the system already being so stressed that it cannot take much more. Adding just a little bit more stress pushes it over the brink into collapse, because something has to give. As more consequences pile up, even more stress is added to the system, which can initiate a destructive downward spiral.

Steel is an interesting substance. It is a metaphor for hardness and strength. *Hard as steel.* An alloy of iron combined with carbon, it can be made as hard as possible by heating it up to red-hotness, and then dunking it suddenly in water (a process called *quenching*). Steel that's been quenched is not only super-hard, but also so brittle that it's practically useless. It shatters almost like glass. So why are there scenes of swordsmiths in every movie quenching their dragon-slaying blades? Because after quenching there is a second step, called *tempering*, which softens the steel slightly by heating it again. Tempering gives the steel an ideal mix of hardness and springiness— the ideal Goldilocks zone for the blacksmith's art. The blade will bend instead of breaking, making it incredibly tough. Perfect for a sword.

Resilience is like just the right amount of springiness in steel. It makes you stronger and yet less brittle, a kind of tempering of your inner steel. Even when life throws you a truly awful body blow, it doesn't knock you out. Like tempered steel, you can bend without breaking. With resilience, you can march through the darkness and pain and emerge on the other side in pretty good shape. Everything you've been learning in this book will go a long way toward cultivating your resilience. But now it's time to enhance your resilience even further using a technique that's a little different than the ones we've already encountered. Done consistently, it can give you perhaps a little of Muad'dib's ability to deal with difficult situations.

When I first introduce students to this technique, called Focus on Positive, there is sometimes a collective groan. Yes, the practice involves intentionally focusing on positive things, which I know is a trigger for some. From movies like *The Secret* and *What the Bleep Do We Know?!*, to books like *Think and Grow Rich* and *The Power of Positive Thinking*, the woo-woo part of our culture never grows tired of celebrating and aggressively marketing a mental state of positivity. Just thinking the right thoughts will, apparently, make you rich, irresistible, and possessed of godlike powers (for a small fee). Toss in some specious quantum mysticism as a pseudo-scientific explanation, and you've got a recipe for a New Age bestseller. It's no wonder that to an audience of mindful geeks, the mere mention of the practice of positive emotions may elicit everything from mild discomfort to derisive sneers.

The trouble is that this snowstorm of marketing hype obscures some fascinating data about the *actual* power of positive thinking and feeling. While it might not teleport a billion-dollar check into your bank account, intentionally cultivating optimism has measurable, real-world effects on your longevity, health, and most importantly on your resilience. Focus on Positive is a very effective way to up your resilience to much higher levels.

Because I feel your skepticism, let's jump right into the intriguing evidence. Most of the studies use a Buddhist practice called "lovingkindness" meditation, which I'm calling Focus on Positive. This is a technique in which you essentially concentrate on wishing people well. It's very easy to do, and the effects are quite interesting, especially in diminishing stress.

Chronic stress, as we've seen, takes a big chunk out of your resilience. It's wearing down the system, little by little, day after day. Practicing the FOP technique has a calming effect on the nervous system, significantly reducing stress. One study[109] found that doing just 10 minutes of it (with no history of practice) increased respiratory sinus arrhythmia (RSA) and decreased respiratory rates in participants, both indicators of relaxation, and another[110] showed clear reduction in the immune and behavioral responses indicative of stress. A more far-reaching study[111] found that women who had done a significant amount of FOP over time had significantly longer telomere length— a key indicator of longevity—compared to controls, even when levels of past trauma and depression were taken into account. And FOP was shown[112] to drastically reduce levels of PTSD and moderately reduce depression in veterans, even three months after they had finished a training course. So clearly doing the Focus on Positive practice can reduce your stress.

People doing seven weeks of FOP boosted a wide range of positive emotions, which in turn produced an increase in personal resources such as improved mindfulness, sense of purpose in life, social support, and decreased illness symptoms.[113] All of these are factors that build resilience. The more personal resources you have are your disposal, the less likely it is that a super-difficult time will deliver you, as Tolkien might put it, a "fell blow." Focus on Positive practice also boosts your "vagal tone," which is a key indicator of health and wellbeing.[114] Because the vagus nerve regulates the body's internal organs, particularly the heart, vagal tone serves as an index of the overall state of the parasympathetic nervous system. The authors of this study go further and postulate that positive emotions lead to better health (which we'll see more about in a moment), which leads to more social connections, and so on in an upward spiral of building resilience factors.

The idea that experiencing positive emotions can actually lead to better health and quicker healing is perhaps the biggest red flag for most people. There is something about medical claims that just screams quackery. But there are solid studies that confirm that cultivating optimism can provide meaningful help with medical issues. For example, the Focus on Positive technique significantly reduced the pain of a migraine headache in subjects (who had never meditated before) after just one 20-minute session.[115] A Duke Medical Center study found that people with chronic lower back pain experienced big improvements in both pain and psychological distress compared to controls.[116] And research from Emory University showed a relationship between time spent practicing Focusing on Positive and a reduction in inflammation and distress in response to stress. One of the researchers commented: "If practicing compassion meditation does reduce inflammatory responses to stress it might offer real promise as a means of preventing many conditions associated with stress and with inflammation including major depression, heart disease and diabetes."[117]

In most of the studies, Focus on Positive not only enhanced wellbeing in a physical sense, but it also helped the person to feel more positive emotions—which is both the goal of the practice and itself a major benefit. If we consider that feeling positive emotions is the main effect of practicing FOP, then we can also consider studies that show the benefits of feeling good emotions.

Think your emotional state doesn't matter much? Just watching a comedy film increases the level of immunoglobulin A in the saliva. One meta-analysis of 30 happiness studies found a very strong relationship between feeling positive emotions and longevity—an effect as large as smoking versus not smoking. The interesting wrinkle is that this was only found in healthy populations. That is, feeling positive seems to help protect you against getting sick, but once you are ill, it doesn't have much effect.[118] Another study showed that among male war veterans, optimists experienced fewer incidents of angina and heart attacks.[119] And a study of elderly heart surgery patients showed that feeling positive emotions predicted a lower re-admission rate, even when controlled for factors such as health status upon release, length of hospital stay, and so on.[120]

So practicing Focusing on Positive and experiencing positive emotions constitute a scientifically solid way to increase your resilience, be healthier, live longer, and—even if all that fails—at least you'll feel much better while you're doing it.

Puppies and Kittehs

Simply put, the Focus on Positive practice involves thinking about nice things, and meditating on the good feelings this generates. In the first part, "thinking about nice things" you picture a specific person who you want to think about, and then you wish for nice things to happen to them. You might picture your mom, say, and then mentally say good things that you hope she experiences. You might mentally say to your mom, "I hope (or wish) that you are happy today. I hope that you feel peaceful. I hope that you feel enough love in your life," and so on.

Try that right now. Just think of your mom (or somebody you really love). Picture her in your mind's eye, feeling all happy and healthy. Then start wishing or hoping that she experience some positive feelings. Do this for a minute or so.

The second part is to experience the good feelings this generates. You do this exactly like you did during the Focus on Emotion practice, with the exception that you're only focusing on *positive* emotions. If none are present, that's OK. In that case, just keep making the positive wishes.

In my experience, most people love this practice. It's easy and it feels good. However, it can also cause some people a bit of difficulty. One common pitfall is if you are the sort of person who can only do it in a sarcastic, cynical, or ironic manner. There's nothing wrong with these moods or stances, but it helps to be able to turn them off occasionally, when you want to.

If you can only encounter this practice ironically, your challenge will be to find something, somewhere, that you can actually have genuine, heartfelt, straightforward good feelings about. Instead of using an adult human being as your focus object, try beginning with a being who is extremely non-threatening and uncomplicated, like a tiny baby or an adorable puppy or kitten. Someone or something that you just cannot have bad feelings about. Feel free to even use a cartoon character, or even an abstract concept like "everyone in the world" or "all my friends" if that works better for you. The good news here is that, with repeated practice, your base level of cynicism will be reduced , so the meditation will get easier to do.

A second pitfall is feeling guilty about experiencing positive emotions. How, you might ask, can you sit there and imagine unicorns, daisies, and sunshine when real children are starving? The earth is choking to death on carbon-rich gases, and there you are, frolicking with imaginary puppies in your mind. There are so many real-world problems to solve, and sitting there wishing things were different isn't going to change anything.

It's not that this viewpoint is untrue, it's just that it's not helpful. If you cannot allow yourself even a half an hour to feel some positive feelings without feeling guilty and maybe even angry, then you may be headed for eventual burnout. People who are the most effective at making positive change in the world make sure that they have downtime to rest, feel good, and relax. They use positive personal experiences to build their resilience so that they don't experience burnout. On the other hand, people whose emotional reaction to the injustices of the world is so intense that it doesn't allow them to ever rest or feel good, cannot sustain a high level of activism for very long. Their chronic upset condition causes them to lose resilience and eventually they are *forced* by fatigue, illness, or dysfunction to finally rest.

If this is your way in life, I strongly encourage you to allow yourself some downtime, at least during a half an hour of meditation practice per day, so that you can fortify your resilience. The Focus on Positive technique will actually help you to make the changes in the world you want to make, because it helps to keep you refreshed and able to work. There is probably no more powerful method to ensure that you can be out there fighting the good fight year after year.

A third pitfall is when people cannot think of positive things without being drawn into a negative quagmire. This may go something like: "But the puppy is a lot like a puppy I saw the other day, which has a genetic disorder and cannot digest. That poor little guy needs an operation for its intestines. It reminded me of my childhood puppy, who got hit by a car. It was the worst experience of my life," and so on. Every train of thought eventually ends up on the tracks headed toward Mordor, and by the end of the meditation, they are even more depressed, fraught, or upset than before.

Partially, this may just be the result of habits of negative thought, but on a deeper level it's the result of *negativity bias*. Negativity bias refers to the fact that human beings cannot help but place our attention upon objects in our environment that appear to be threatening. All other things being equal, we are much more likely to pay attention to potential threats than to potential benefits.

The reason for this imbalance is the "better safe than sorry" aspect of natural selection. In terms of survival, the cost for doing something wrong is very high—such as death. The benefit for doing something right, on the other hand, is simply continuing onward. Add this up over hundreds of millions of years of evolution, and it means that your brain is very, very interested in registering potentially dangerous stimuli. This selection mechanism has been at work in animals since the beginning of time, and humans are no exception. We are programmed by evolution to have a bias toward negative information, meaning that we find scary, dangerous stuff much more interesting than positive, happy information. We may not like it, but we're helplessly fascinated by it.

It's much easier for most of us to fantasize about difficult, awful stuff rather than pleasant, upbeat stuff. Noticing this is an insight, and represents a little peek under the hood of how your brain operates. Being caught up in a never ending negative story is not good for your health, your work, your state of mind, or those around you. Yes, it's important to be realistic and not fall into a Pollyannaish, head-in-the-sand lifestyle. We all have to be clear about the real problems and challenges in the world. But if you are experiencing any of the above pitfalls in your Focus on Positive practice, you are *not* one of the Pollyannas in the world. In fact, you may fall more on the Cassandra side of the midpoint. So you are not in danger of becoming too blithely positive. You are, in fact, only in danger of feeling good and experiencing some wellbeing.

FOCUS ON POSITIVE – GUIDED PRACTICE

Before you begin, find your meditation seat, either sitting in a chair, on a bench, a cushion, or the floor.

Sit up straight, extending your spine upwards toward the ceiling. Make sure your chin is pointing just slightly (5 degrees) below horizontal.

Next relax your entire body. Take three deep breaths, and let each one of them out long and slowly.

Now you're ready to begin the Focus on Positive practice.

Begin by thinking of somebody you love. It can be your mother, your partner, or anybody else. Make sure it is someone that you don't have complicated or difficult feelings about. It can even be a fictional character. For this example, we'll use Yoda.

Picture Yoda having the greatest day of his life. See him clearly in your mind's eye as happy and joyful as a Jedi Master can be. See him jumping up and down, spinning in circles, playing with his friends, eating his favorite foods, and anything else that seems like it would make him feel fabulous. Maybe he's just smiling enigmatically, looking at a sunset.

At the same time mentally say things in the form of a series of wishes or statements of intention, such as, "I wish that you be happy. I wish that you be healthy. I wish that you have peace in your life." and so on. You can say "I hope" rather than "I wish," or say these any other way that appeals to you. Just wish Yoda well in lots of ways.

For example:

I wish that you be happy.
I wish that you be healthy.
I wish that you have peace in your life.
I wish that you know joy.
I wish that you know love.
I wish that you have lots of friends.
I wish that you know safety.

And so on.

Keep seeing happy Yoda, while saying these things to him mentally. As you're doing this, be careful not to slip into any negative feelings ("This is silly. He's a foam rubber puppet."). Instead, guide your visualization by checking in every so often with emotional body sensation. Make sure that you're building up happy, joyous, grateful feelings. If negative feelings are happening, try to gently steer the visualizations in a more positive direction. If no feelings are happening at all, that's fine.

Keep doing this for 3-5 minutes. Give it your best effort. Build up a charge of positive emotional sensations, if you can.

When the time is up, let go of the intentional creation of mental images and mental talk. Shift your attention completely to emotional body sensation. Locate only positive emotional sensations, and do your meditation algorithm on them. Really allow awareness to "soak into" these feelings. Do this until any positive sensations have gone back to neutral, or whenever you feel done.

You have completed one round. Now start the visualization again and do another round.

Continue with this for as many or as few rounds as you like.

When it's time to finish, spend at least one minute just sitting quietly, meditating on pleasant sensations in the body before continuing on your day.

VARIATIONS

1. By far the most important variation of this exercise is to do it for *yourself*. Because this is often harder for people than doing it for another, I don't usually start people there. Many Americans have a difficult time simply generating some positive emotions about themselves. It is, however, a very effective way to build resilience. So if you can handle wishing yourself well as a meditation, then by all means dig in.

2. Try doing Focus on Positive for a person you are currently in conflict with. If you and your romantic partner, for example, are having a hard time, dedicate a half an hour of FOP for them. You may be surprised how effective this is at overcoming seemingly insurmountable relationship problems. Unless you are fairly experienced and comfortable with this practice, however, I wouldn't recommend doing it for a person who you actually don't like. That's an advanced practice, because it easily can devolve into a negative experience.

CHAPTER TWENTY THREE
Heaven Is Other People

In the episode of *Star Trek: The Next Generation* entitled, "I, Borg," the crew of the Enterprise discover a crashed scout vessel on the surface of a small moon. In the wreckage is a number of dead Borg drones, and one unconscious survivor—known as "Third of Five." Taking the drone back to the Enterprise, a conflict among the crew erupts around whether to heal his wounds. Worf insists they kill him at once. Dr. Crusher is adamant that he be treated like any other patient, which makes Picard—a personal victim of the Borg collective— furious. Data devises a plan to heal Third of Five, then plant a sort of computer virus in him and send him back to the collective as a weapon of mass destruction.

Soon the conflict grows more intense, as Geordi nicknames the drone "Hugh" and spends more and more time talking to him. Hugh stops referring to himself using the pronoun "we," and switches to "I," telling Geordi that he is lonely; he misses the hive. When the bartender/alien Guinan (played by Whoopi Goldberg) talks to Hugh, telling him that her entire civilization was wiped out by the Borg, Hugh responds by recognizing that she, Guinan is lonely, too. He demonstrates a surprising emotion for a Borg drone: empathy. Guinan is shocked. Even Picard becomes convinced that Hugh is an individual, and gives up on the plan to genocide the Borg. Thus

Hugh's empathy not only saves himself, but the entire Borg collective.

When we as a society want to punish a person, we stick them in prison. But when we want to punish someone who is already incarcerated, we do something strange: put him or her alone in a cell without human contact. Prisons are crowded, dangerous places, packed to the rafters with violent criminals. You'd think that getting put in your own private cell would be seen as some kind of reward. But instead solitary confinement is universally reviled by prisoners as one of the worst things that can happen to you, and human rights advocates insist that it is actually a form of torture.[121] Just like the Borg drone Hugh, we can't stand being alone all the time.

The reason for this is that human beings evolved to live in groups, to hunt and gather food in groups, to eat and sleep in groups, and to coordinate and cooperate as a group. As far back as the archeological digs go, whenever you find a camp of humans or proto-humans, they exist in a group, a tribe, a clan. Evolution has selected us, over long millions of years, to be *profoundly social*. This doesn't mean that we like to be in groups, it means that, in some sense, we cannot be fully human without ongoing group contact. Groups of humans can almost be thought of as constituting a sort of hive organism, like the Borg.

Unlike the Borg, however, human beings didn't evolve to use cranial transceivers to communicate and organize our social units. We use emotional expressions and language to do that. By emotional expressions, I mean things like scowling or blushing or smiling. As Darwin himself pointed out in his bestselling 1872 book *The Expression of Emotion in Man and Animals*, our facial expressions evolved from their animal precursors as ways to communicate our internal state to our fellows. Especially before the advent of articulate spoken language, emotional expressions were perhaps our chief mode of communication for working as a team and maintaining group cohesion. In earlier chapters, we already looked at how to meditate on emotions.

Another specially evolved feature in humans is the capacity for empathy and compassion, or what biologists like to call altruism.[122] On the face of it, Darwinian natural selection would seem to rule out the possibility of altruism becoming a lasting feature in a species, since the most selfish individuals would eventually become dominant in the population. The more they ripped off the altruism of the nice guys, the more they would thrive. Meanwhile the do-gooders would slowly die out. Theories such as *kin selection*—the idea that helping out relatives means helping individuals who share a large portion of our DNA—have been proposed to resolve this apparent conundrum.

The question remains a hotly contested one in biology, but what is not disputed is that human beings do exhibit altruistic behavior and have done so for a very long time. The signs of ancient compassion are there in the fossil record. There is a fossil individual with a severely deformed skull, who could only have lived to his apparent age through the care of others. There is another individual who lost all use of his right arm, was likely blind and deaf, and limped as well. He lived with these infirmities a long time, and yet this would've only been possible if the other adults were assisting him. There is a lot of other fossil evidence of altruism.[123] Apparently we've been helping each other out since our brains were half the size that they are today.

Our brains may even have evolved special neurons that help us be more empathic and to facilitate our understanding of other people. Primate brains possess a special type of neuron that fires when it sees *another* primate take an action. One monkey eats a peanut, and a spectator monkey's brain make a signal as if *it's* eating a peanut. These are called "mirror neurons," and we are not yet certain whether they exist in human beings, but the evidence from several different studies seems to indicate that they do. When we see another person doing something, mirror neurons reflect that behavior in our own brains. By experiencing their movement and gestures ourselves, we "feel our way" into understanding another person's internal state. This is how we form a mental model about what other people may be thinking and feeling. Many researchers contend that mirror neurons constitute an important neural mechanism for empathy. And our empathy beings can be intense. A recent study[124] from the University of Virginia showed that the pain of our friends is almost indistinguishable from our own pain.

The Down Side

Living in groups probably contributed greatly to survival for our ancient ancestors. Through cooperation and caring for each other, they formed a cohesive group that was stronger by far than any of the individual members alone. Our sociality can be seen as humanity's secret weapon; the superhero power that helped us to conquer the planet. Like all superhero powers, however, there is a hidden downside: our need for social connection means that loneliness and isolation have a profoundly negative impact on our health and wellbeing.

Using the new science of social genomics, for example, UCLA researchers John Cappioco and Steve Cole have discovered that loneliness actually alters gene expression in the immune system. Our immune system has a limited capacity for defense, and is forced to "decide" between optimizing to fight either bacterial or viral threats. In lonely people, immune system genes for fighting bacterial invasion are over-expressed, and the ones for combatting viruses are under-expressed. That puts these people at risk for cancer and other diseases, which is confirmed by a wealth[125] of research. The authors speculate that in groups there is more of a chance of viral disease vectors, which is why the non-lonely immune system optimizes in that direction.

Furthermore, some of the over-expressed genes in lonely people cause higher blood levels of cortisol (the main hormone implicated in the stress response), leading to greater risk of heart attacks, strokes, high blood pressure, and blood vessel damage.[126] The researchers trace these influences to the fact that prehistoric people living in isolation were in grave danger, and thus loneliness produces a state of stress, an emotional signal to direct the individual back toward the safety of the group.

A 2015 meta-analysis by Brigham Young University examined the impact on mortality of loneliness, social isolation, and living alone, and the results are sobering.[127] Looking at almost 35 years of research on more than three million subjects, they found that these forms of isolation increased the risk of mortality—i.e. early death—by 26, 29, and 32 percent respectively. That is, being lonely and isolated makes you about *one-third more likely to die young*, a finding that remained consistent regardless of gender, length of follow-up, or world region. As Julianne Holt-Lunstad, the lead researcher commented, "We need to start taking our social relationships more seriously. The effect of this is comparable to obesity, something that public health takes very seriously."

But the really compelling fact about this study is that they found no difference in the mortality effect between actual isolation and feelings of loneliness. That is, it doesn't matter whether you are actually alone or just that you feel isolated, the impact on your longevity is the same. A person surrounded by a crowd, but who feels alone, is just as at risk as a person who never leaves the house. This is the source of a potentially life-changing, or in this case life-saving, possibility. Because if Focus on Positive meditation can increase our feelings of belonging and social support simply by imagining them, that's just as powerful as having actual belonging and social connections, at least in terms of health. Building a social support system for someone who doesn't have it is worth doing, but it is time-consuming, dependent on mobility and location factors, personality, opportunity, and a number of other challenges. Just sitting down and doing some Focus on Positive meditation, on the other hand, is quick, easy, free, and virtually risk-free, and anyone can practice it.

Enter Oxytocin

Another aspect of humans beings' sociality is that we have evolved specific hormones to help us interact with each other more smoothly. Probably the most celebrated such hormone is *oxytocin*, which has become the subject of intense interest in last decade. Oxytocin is deeply involved in the biology of childbirth (it causes uterine contractions and lactation, among other things), but has also been found to play an important role in human social and sexual bonding. This feature has excited the minds of journalists, who never seem to tire of giving it catchy nicknames like the "love hormone," the "cuddle hormone," and even the "moral molecule."

And, indeed, oxytocin has some very attractive qualities. It's released when we cuddle each other, and increases trust,[128] empathy,[129] generosity,[130] and promotes social bonding. Mice who were genetically engineered to lack oxytocin treated mice they had met before like strangers.[131] Humans who received a dose of oxytocin spray in their nose (the common method used in many studies) showed increased memory for social information[132] and the faces of others.[133] Oxytocin is released during sexual intercourse and orgasm,[134] helps couples bond,[135] and even functions to keep males faithful in monogamous relationships.[136] If you want to have satisfying social, parental, and sexual relationships—all important factors in overall wellbeing—oxytocin would seem to play a key role. Predictably, the ever-excited journalists have also dubbed it the "tend and befriend" hormone.

If that moniker reminds you of the name of the "fight or flight" mechanism, it's no coincidence. Researchers have found that the tend-and-befriend circuit functions, in a way, as the opposite of the fight or flight circuit. Oxytocin down-regulates the HPA[137] (axis of the fight-or-flight mechanism), inhibits the amygdala[138] (thereby reducing fear), suppresses cortisol,[139] and increases feelings of calm and contentment. So it directly (under most conditions) helps you to chill out and let go of stress. There's even evidence that oxytocin reduces inflammation factors in the blood which promotes the speedy healing of wounds.[140] Does this mean that when mommy "kisses it" it really does "make it better"?

As of this writing, there is no direct evidence that meditation practice increases oxytocin. However, there are some intriguing hints that this probably is the case. For one, just watching a short emotionally stimulating movie can raise oxytocin levels as much as 47 percent.[141] It seems like the brain doesn't distinguish carefully between empathy for an actual human and empathy for an image of a human being. Thus when we imagine feeling close to others in the Focus on Positive technique, it's likely that the same mechanism kicks in and increases oxytocin.[142]

Human beings are exquisitely tuned by evolution to care for each other. Not only does the care we give help others, but it also directly helps ourselves. When we care about healing others, it heals us. When we want others to feel better, we feel better, too. Encouraging others to feel safe and calm encourages us to feel safe and calm. The Focus on Positive technique leverages this built-in tend-and-befriend feedback to boost your resilience to higher and higher levels. Give it a try for just a week, and see what happens to your mood.

CHAPTER TWENTY FOUR

The Brain's Screensaver

Remember when Seti@home was a thing? SETI stands for the Search for Extraterrestrial Intelligence, and it's the organization featured in the movie *Contact*, using radio telescopes to search the skies for stray signals from unknown alien civilizations. The idea of Seti@home was to use your computer's idle cycles to help SETI analyze all that radio telescope data. As long as a computer is running, it is still working, even if you are not doing anything with it. Somebody realized that millions of computers around the world were just sitting there, on but unused, half of the day and all night long. What if they could put all that wasted computer resource power to use? SETI designed a program that would be triggered when the computer switched to idle mode, just like screen saver.

It was a big hit, and led to a huge number of copycat projects. Probably the most interesting of these was Folding@home, which used computer idle time to calculate various folding arrangements for proteins. Protein folding is a critical feature in organic biology, but it is extraordinarily complicated, each protein having an astronomical number of ways it can fold. By farming out the folding algorithms to tens of thousands of computers, the Folding@home project contributed to several scientific discoveries, and is currently working on studying proteins related to Alzheimer's and Huntington's disease.[143]

During its downtime, a computer can still be doing something very useful, like finding the cures for diseases, or perhaps discovering advanced alien life forms. But what is the human brain doing during its downtime? Does the brain have a screen saver mode? Some of the most exciting current neuroscience looks into the question of what the brain does when it's not involved in any particular task. There are colloquial terms for this state of mind, like "daydreaming" or being "checked out," but in neuroscience it's called "mind wandering." Through the use of fMRI, scientists have discovered that there is a specific brain network dedicated to this mode of processing. And in a fascinating experiment, they found out something surprising: *most of us are checked out about half of the time.*[144]

In an experiment that I referenced earlier, Harvard scientists Matthew Killingsworth and Daniel Gilbert created an iPhone app that sent participants messages at random intervals a few times a day. The messages prompted users to answer an online survey which asked (1) what they were doing (they could choose from a list of about 20 items), (2) whether they were thinking about that activity or about something else, and (3) how they were feeling emotionally (on a scale of 0-100). Over 5000 individuals participated, and the response rate was quite high, with people answering the messages over 80 percent of the time. After correcting for a number of factors that might have skewed the data, Killingsworth and Gilbert had records for 2250 adults to analyze.

They discovered that people's minds are wandering an amazing *47 percent of the time.* That's right, people are daydreaming—thinking about something completely unrelated—about half the time, no matter what activity they were involved in. (Except sex, when it was wandering "only" 30 percent of the time. But then again, these people chose to answer their iPhone during sex.) The data revealed something important to us in terms of wellbeing: people were on average *least happy during mind wandering,* and this was true no matter what activity they were doing. Hence the title of Killingsworth and Gilbert's article, "A Wandering Mind Is an Unhappy Mind."

So daydreaming often bums you out, and paying attention to the present moment tends to make you feel good. You might actually feel better concentrating on a unpleasant moment in the present, than daydreaming about having sex with your favorite fantasy person. The Harvard experiment lends weight to the effective of mindfulness meditation in improving wellbeing, since the idea of meditation is to stay focused on the present moment. And there is solid research[145] to demonstrate that meditation, by keeping your attention centered in the present moment, reduces your mind wandering. I've heard many meditation teachers over the years say that even having a hard, emotionally fraught meditation session was better than not meditating at all. I always wondered if that was just a platitude to help students make it through a chewing-on-rocks type of sit, but this study (and others) would suggest that their advice was right on target.

Scientists have discovered that there is a brain network associated with mind wandering, and have named it the *default mode network* (DMN), since mind wandering seems to be our default setting. We experience it subjectively as a stream of memories, plans, and fantasies, mostly centered around ourselves and our personal concerns. A soundtrack of it might go something like, "I shouldn't have said that to her last night. So stupid. That reminds me of a date I had in high school, when I took my girlfriend out in Dad's Jeep. I've always wanted to buy a new Jeep like that. Blue. First I'll have to get a better job..." and so on, ad nauseam. Often these words are accompanied by internal images as well. Mental pictures of the date, of the Jeep, of Dad, and so forth.

So the default mode is like a never-ending reality TV show starring ourselves, in which we ruminate on things that happened in the past, and things that may happen in the future. To describe it generously, we might say that the default mode network is concerned with evaluating the outcomes of past actions and using that as a basis for planning future actions. In fact, such evaluation and planning is probably the intended function of the default mode network in the brain. More often, however, it's the mode in which we beat ourselves up over things from the distant past that we can't change, and worry ourselves sick about future events that will never occur. Mark Twain's snarky remark; "I've had a lot of worries in my life, most of which never happened," serves as a perfect description of DMN activity. For most of us the DMN is the nexus of negative, self-referential anxiety and depression.

Default mode network activity is roughly the opposite of a flow state. In a flow state, you begin to lose your sense of self in a task; most thought is self-referential in the DMN. A flow state is intrinsically rewarding and serene, whereas mind wandering typically leaves you feeling bad. The essence of a flow state is concentrated activity; the DMN turns on when you are not focused on any activity. In fact, DMN activity is so closely associated with not paying attention that scientists found that they could use it to predict people making a mistake on a concentration task almost thirty seconds in advance—just by measuring an increase in DMN activity.[146]

The discovery of the DMN has raised a number of very interesting questions about the human brain. For one thing, it suggests that the brain is never actually at rest. As a child, I thought that people's brains just shut off while sleeping, sort of like turning off the TV. And something like this was the scientific view of the brain for a long time. But actually your brain is just about as active (something like +/- 5 percent) while you're sleeping as when you're awake.[147] Think about that for a moment: that's like saying that your car uses almost as much gas when it's parked in the garage with the engine turned off as when you're driving at 70 MPH down the highway. How is that even possible? The answer seems to be what I've been suggesting throughout this book, which is that it is the unconscious—the activity of the brain normally unavailable to conscious introspection—doing all the heavy lifting below conscious awareness. That means that when you're asleep, and consciousness is diminished or absent, it doesn't really subtract from overall brain activity that much, because the unconscious mind is still hard at work. In essence, your brain is always going 70 MPH down the highway, whether you're asleep or not.

A second question revolves around the fact that studies have shown that increased activity and connectivity in the DMN is directly correlated with difficult mental afflictions, such as such as depression, anxiety, addiction, and obsession.[148] The mind-wandering state really is an unhappy one, generally. But if the DMN is associated with such distressing conditions, why would it have evolved to be the normal mode of the brain? It seems unlikely (although not impossible) that evolution would have selected for mental illness in humans. Are we hardwired to be unhappy?

The answer is probably related to the DMN's role in planning. The advanced capacity for prognostication was a tremendous survival advantage for our hominid ancestors. Humans can make detailed plans for things that are years away in time and miles away in space. It's what has allowed us to become the dominant species on this planet. However, we don't live in the simple savannah environment we evolved to survive in. As our technology and societies have grown more and more complex, it may be that the DMN now has a bit too much work to do. The complexity of our current environment requires a quantity and intricacy of planning that is likely far beyond anything ever needed in the past. So it's not that evolution selected for mental illness, it's that we didn't evolve to live in a world this labyrinthine, entangled, and interconnected. There are so many variables and contingencies that the planning function in your brain just has too much to deal with. Have you ever laid awake at night just planning and planning and planning? This unfortunate condition is probably not going to go away anytime soon, since society and technology seem to be getting ever more complex each year. Luckily, meditation allows you to correct for this over-activity by purposefully down-regulating the DMN, as we'll see.

Unsurprisingly, given its function, the DMN also seems to play a role in creativity, since planning future actions involves creative thinking. In fact, the cortical regions of the default mode network are physically thicker in creative individuals[149], and having an active DMN does appear to be important in creativity.[150] This connection to creativity, however, brings up a third interesting question: Does that mean that meditation—which switches off the DMN—is bad for creativity?

Fortunately, there is a ton of other research that demonstrates that mindfulness meditation is also great for boosting creativity.[151] What accounts for this apparent contradiction? The jury is still out on this question, but the answer may be that it depends on *how much effort you're using to meditate*. Paying attention doesn't have to be a chore. When you allow meditation to come from a place of curiosity and interest, paying attention becomes much easier, and a flow state can arise. It is this effortless state that is associated with creativity, whether in DMN activity or meditation.

In his 1926 classic on creativity, *The Art of Thought*, Graham Wallas suggested a four-stage model of the creative process in human beings: preparation, incubation, illumination, and verification. You probably have heard of the main idea of Wallas's model, which is to take a break from problem solving in order to "let your unconscious mind work on it." It is during this "incubation" phase that we solve creative challenges by *letting go of making an effort*. Although this book is long out of print, his theory has not only become the basis of all modern teachings on creativity, it has been mathematically modeled and reproduced using a computer.[152] Essentially, by letting go of effort and relaxing away from trying, we solve creative problems. As neuroscientist and meditation researcher Judson Brewer puts it in an article exploring the connection between meditation and creativity, "effortlessness may be a key aspect of cultivating the fertile soil for creativity to grow.[153]"

This connection with effortlessness gives you a pointer about a way to increase the power of your meditation practice in general. Brewer studies the DMN extensively, and has found (along with others) that the less effort you expend in meditation, the more powerfully you switch off the DMN and the easier it is to enter a flow state.[154]

Although all meditation practices seek to bring us into the present moment, there is a case to be made that the more effortless a practice is, the more effective it is at focusing us in the Now and inducing a flow state. Effortlessness may be key, and it turns out that there are meditation practices specifically designed to exploit this fact.

So far in this book we've been working with a sort of concentration called "focused attention," meaning that you put your awareness on one spot and try to keep it there. If it moves from that focus object, you bring it back. But there is a second kind of attention in which you don't try to control which object you're paying attention to at all. You allow your attention to wander wherever it likes. This second kind of attention is called "open awareness," or "choiceless awareness." The most important feature of open awareness is that *it feels effortless*.

You may well ask how this can even be called a kind of concentration at all. It doesn't sound much different from rank mind wandering. However, there is one important difference, and that is that you are paying close attention to whatever object awareness is resting on at the moment. So you don't care what your focus object is—in a sense, you could say that in this way of working, *everything* is a potential focus object—but you're giving your full attention to whatever thing awareness just happens to rest on, moment by moment. Because you're constantly in touch with whatever's arising, you're staying in close contact with the present moment. But because you're not trying to keep your mind focused on any particular object, and not bringing it back over and over to that object, it feels effortless.

Because of this sense of effortlessness, open awareness is a powerful and practical way not only to contact the present moment, but also to reduce default mode network activation. If you want to enter a flow state, this is a great way to do it. All it takes to shut down DMN activity and go into a flow state is to concentrate on a task. The task doesn't have to be useful or even make sense, it just has to engage you in the present moment. And the meditation technique you're about to learn is perfect for doing that.

Letting Go of Effort

In this book, we'll call open awareness the Focus on Now technique, and the instructions are simple: allow your attention to go wherever it wants, and just notice whatever comes up. That's it. Do not try to direct your attention at all. Another way to give the same instructions (and this is the way Shinzen describes it) is to let go of all effort. If anything feels like you're trying to do something, let go of doing that. No matter how you describe it, the essence is the same: you are paying attention, but not to anything in particular. You are letting go of any sense of *trying to do.*

Of course, even paying attention and letting go may require a little bit of effort. The goal here is to let go of as much effort as possible, not to judge yourself for not having reached the absolute zero of effort.

While the instructions for the Focus on Now technique are simple, ironically it's not always that easy to do. When it's going well, this meditation is very pleasurable, having all the intrinsic benefits of a flow state without even the typical focus-object a flow state requires. It's like learning to have a flow state on everything or nothing at all.

When it's not going so well, it can feel like you're bored and restless, without even the relief of having something to concentrate on. It's possible to get caught up in thinking, or get assailed by thoughts, and to feel like you have no defense from all this monkey-mind madness. Getting relief from such chaos is often one of the reasons people start meditating in the first place. It sometimes helps to frame the Focus on Now practice as a strong acceptance meditation, because to sit and allow almost anything to unfold in meditation is a deeply accepting stance to take. Everything that arises, everything that occurs in your senses is fine. Everything. You're just going to stay with it, no matter what it is.

No matter what, it's important that you do this meditation as with as light a touch as possible. As much as you can, let go of the sense of effort, of trying. You may not be able to let go 100 percent, but 25 percent is fine. Even if all you can let go is one percent, that's a good start. The more you can let go of the sense of effort, the deeper you sink into the flow of this meditation.

FOCUS ON NOW – GUIDED PRACTICE

Before you begin, find your meditation seat, either sitting in a chair, on a bench, a cushion, or the floor.

Sit up straight, extending your spine upwards toward the ceiling. Make sure your chin is pointing just slightly (5 degrees) below horizontal.

Next relax your entire body. Take three deep breaths, and let each one of them out long and slowly.

Now you're ready to begin the Focus on Now practice.

Lightly focus on your meta-attention; the thing that tells you what you're focusing on right now.

Now just allow your attention to notice any aspect of the present moment. It doesn't matter what it is. Just notice, using your meta-attention, that attention is pointed at some aspect of the present. Just sit with that.

If meta-attention tells you that attention has left the present moment, bring it back. Do this as gently, softly, and kindly as you can.

Try to do this meditation with as little sense of doing anything as possible. You are simply sitting and noticing where attention is going, and gently bringing it back to the present moment.

Continue with this for as long as you like. When it's time to finish, spend at least one minute just sitting quietly, meditating on relaxed sensations in the body before continuing on your day.

CHAPTER TWENTY FIVE

Ready?

You have learned five different meditation techniques in this book. You may be wondering how to practically deal with them all. The short version is that it's up to you. If there is one technique that you like more than the others, just concentrate on doing that one for the time being. Someday one of the other ones may begin to appeal to you, and you can feel free to pick that one up then. Another possibility is that you might want to do all of them, which also works. You could, for example, just iterate through the five of them, one per day. That's also a fine strategy. They are all building concentration, sensory clarity, and acceptance in varying degrees, and so they all are building a common set of skills. The only way that I *don't* recommend you use them is all together in one sitting. Restrict each session of meditation to just one technique. Otherwise you can end up with a kind of psychological indigestion, so to speak, and not make optimal progress. Just do one at a time.

About Meditation Apps

In the past few years, a slew of apps for meditation have appeared. These do things like time and record your sits, and maybe connect you to other meditators. Sometimes they have teaching courses and sometimes they are "gamified." In general, I think these are absolutely awesome. Because my friends and colleagues develop meditation apps, however, and also because they are changing so quickly, I don't want to recommend any particular one(s) here. Suffice it to say that it won't be difficult for you to find one and begin using it.

In my opinion, these devices are still in their infancy. Soon they will be hooked up with extremely powerful neurofeedback devices, which will help you guide yourself into deep meditation states quickly and accurately. Some of these gadgets already exist, but I cannot wait for them to become much more powerful and accurate. After many thousands of years of meditating in the "old" style (taught in this book), we will soon enter a whole new era of meditation. I think this coming change promises to make meditation much easier and help people to get the benefits much more quickly. That is my hope.

Outro

Finishing a book is such a strange experience. You set out with excitement about the topic, passion for the ideas, and the commitment to creating something that will truly be useful. It's a beautiful dream. And then you struggle for months and years to create your opus, the culmination and consummation of all that energy. And yet, when it's done, it seems like such a little thing; small and pedestrian. There is so much that I want to share with you about meditation, so much to teach and to say. I feel like I could write a thousand more pages and still not begin to get to it all.

But, at the same time, I feel that we've reached a good stopping place. You are ready. You know enough to have a powerful, daily meditation practice that has a very good chance of significantly improving your wellbeing. Yes, there is more to know, more ways to grow, even deeper levels of the unconscious to bring to consciousness, but let's take this one solid step at a time. If you want a sneak preview into the sort of life-changing psychological topics I'll be covering in the follow-up to *The Mindful Geek*, take a look at Sam Harris's excellent book, *Waking Up*.

The path forward is a simple one: meditate every day that you can. Sit 30 minutes every day if that's possible, or at least 10 minutes if that's all you have time for. You can do it at the same time every day, or at random times throughout the day. You can always sit in the same spot, or sit in a new spot every day. Suit yourself. Only be sure that you make it a regular practice, something that becomes a predictable element of your daily life. You can also bring meditative awareness to other parts of your day as you walk around.

As you grow in your practice, it helps to have teachers. There are many teachers and classes available, although most of them will not be secular. If you don't mind being exposed to spiritual teachings and belief systems, there are a large number of mindfulness meditation centers and teachers in almost every city. If you want to stay strictly in a secular humanist mode, skeptical and scientific, then feel free to contact me directly for lessons, or come to one of my online video courses. You can find a current schedule of these at themindfulgeek.net. If you live in the Bay Area, I teach classes in person.

Lastly, I'm very interested in getting constructive feedback about this book. I consider the book to be in beta, and would like to substantially improve it, with your input. If you have questions, comments, additions, corrections, want to report a typo, or feel that something needs clarifying, please feel free to comment in the forum for book feedback on themindfulgeek.net. You can also email me at feedback@themindfulgeek.net. It's very helpful if you make it clear what chapter and paragraph you're talking about, and remember that page numbers are meaningless in digital editions. I look forward to hearing from you.

Endnotes

1 shinzen.org

2 basicmindfulness.org

3 beinghuman.org

4 MacLean, K. A., Ferrer, E., Aichele, S. R., Bridwell, D. A., Zanesco, A. P., Jacobs, T. L., & King, B. G. (2010, June 6). Intensive Meditation Training Improves Perceptual Discrimination and Sustained Attention. Retrieved from http://pss.sagepub.com/content/early/2010/05/11/0956797610371339.abstract

For the record, this study involves individuals practicing five hours a day for three months—a very intense level of commitment. However, there is a lot of research that shows similar if lesser effects for a smaller time commitment.

5 Moore, A., & Malinowski, P. (2009, March 18). Meditation, mindfulness and cognitive flexibility. - PubMed - NCBI. Retrieved from http://www.ncbi.nlm.nih.gov/pubmed/19181542

6 Again, this study involves intensive meditation practice:
Moore, A., & Malinowski, P. (2009, March 18). Meditation, mindfulness and cognitive flexibility. - PubMed - NCBI. Retrieved from http://www.ncbi.nlm.nih.gov/pubmed/19181542

7 Slagter, H. A., Lutz, A., Greischar, L. L., Francis, A. D., Nieuwenhuis, S., Davis, J. M., & Davidson, R. J. (2007, May 8). PLOS Biology: Mental Training Affects Distribution of Limited Brain Resources. Retrieved from http://journals.plos.org/plosbiology/article?id=10.1371/journal.pbio.0050138

8 Paulus, H. E., Williams HJ., M. J., Ward, J. R., & Williams, H. J. (1990, April). Analysis of improvement in individual rheumatoid arthritis patients treated with disease-modifying antirheumatic drugs, based on the findings in pa... - PubMed - NCBI. Retrieved from http://www.ncbi.nlm.nih.gov/pubmed/2109613

9 The Effects of Mindfulness Meditation Training on Multitasking in a High-Stress Information Environment. (n.d.). *Graphics Interface Conference*, 45-52. Retrieved from http://faculty.washington.edu/wobbrock/pubs/gi-12.02.pdf

10 This is a long-term study on people doing an intensive meditation retreat. We'll look at the ample evidence of mindfulness's effect on acute stressors in the Stress Chapter.

Fell, A. (2013, March 27). Mindfulness from meditation associated with lower stress hormone :: UC Davis News & Information. Retrieved from http://www.news.ucdavis.edu/search/news_detail.lasso?id=10538

11 Hofmann, S. G., Sawyer, A. T., Witt, A. A., & Oh, D. (2010, April). The Effect of Mindfulness-Based Therapy on Anxiety and Depression: A Meta-Analytic Review. Retrieved from http://www.ncbi.nlm.nih.gov/pmc/articles/PMC2848393/

12 Sundquist, J., Lilja, A., Palmér, K., Ashfaque A. Memon, A. A., Wang, X., Johansson, L. M., & Sundquist, K. (2014, November). Mindfulness group therapy in primary care patients with depression, anxiety and stress and adjustment disorders: randomised controlled trial | The British Journal of Psychiatry. Retrieved from http://bjp.rcpsych.org/content/early/2014/11/11/bjp.bp.114.150243.abstract?sid=2ca25130-f938-4bf1-835f-4aeb534be010

13 Lutz, A., Brefczynski-Lewis, J., Johnstone, T., & Davidson, R. J. (2008, March 26). PLOS ONE: Regulation of the Neural Circuitry of Emotion by Compassion Meditation: Effects of Meditative Expertise. Retrieved from http://www.plosone.org/article/info%3Adoi%2F10.1371%2Fjournal.pone.0001897

14 Davis, D. M. (2012, August). What are the benefits of mindfulness. Retrieved from http://www.apa.org/monitor/2012/07-08/ce-corner.aspx

15 Ortner, C. N., Kilner, S. J., & Zelazo, P. D. (2007). Mindfulness meditation and reduced emotional interference on a cognitive task. Mo44tivation and Emotion, 271-283. doi:10.1007/s11031-007-9076-7

16 This study particularly refers to "compassion meditation," which we'll look at later in the book under the name Focus on Positive.

Lutz, A., Brefczynski-Lewis, J., Johnstone, T., & Davidson, R. J. (2008, March 26). PLOS ONE: Regulation of the Neural Circuitry of Emotion by Compassion Meditation: Effects of Meditative Expertise. Retrieved from http://journals.plos.org/plosone/article?id=10.1371/journal.pone.0001897

17 Moore, A., & Malinowski, P. (2009, March). Meditation, mindfulness and cognitive flexibility. Retrieved from http://www.sciencedirect.com/science/article/pii/S1053810008001967

18 Ostafin, B. D., & Kassman, K. T. (2012, July 21). Stepping out of history: mindfulness improves insight problem solving. - PubMed - NCBI. Retrieved from http://www.ncbi.nlm.nih.gov/pubmed/22483682

19 Colzato,, L. S., Ozturk,, A., & Hommel, B. (2012, April 18). Meditate to Create: The Impact of Focused-Attention and Open-Monitoring Training on Convergent and Divergent Thinking. Retrieved from http://www.ncbi.nlm.nih.gov/pmc/articles/PMC3328799/

20 Jha, A. P., Stanley, E. A., Kiyonaga, A., Wong, L., & Gelfand, L. (2010). Examining the Protective Effects of Mindfulness Training on Working Memory Capacity and Affective Experience. *Emotion*, *10*(1), 54-64. doi:10.1037/a0018438

21 Franklin, M. S., Phillips, D. T., & Baird, B. (2013, March 26). Brief Mindfulness Training May Boost Test Scores, Working Memory. Retrieved from http://www.psychologicalscience.org/index.php/news/releases/brief-mindfulness-training-may-boost-test-scores-working-memory.html

22 Zeidan, F., Johnson, S. K., Diamond, B. J., David, Z., & Goolkasian, P. (2010). Mindfulness meditation improves cognition: Evidence of brief mental training. *Consciousness and Cognition*, *1*(1), 1-9. doi:10.1016/j.concog.2010.03.014

23 Lazar, S. W., Kerr, C. E., Wasserman, R. H., Gray, J. R., Greve, D. N., Treadway, M. T., & McGarvey, M. (2005, November 28). Meditation experience is associated with increased cortical thickness. Retrieved from http://www.ncbi.nlm.nih.gov/pmc/articles/PMC1361002/

24 Lazar, S. W., Kerr, C. E., Wasserman,, R. H., Gray, J. R., Greve, D. N., Treadway, M. T., & McGarvey, M. (2005, November 28). Cortical thickness and pain sensitivity in zen meditators. - PubMed - NCBI. Retrieved from http://www.ncbi.nlm.nih.gov/pubmed/20141301

25 Lazar, S. W., Kerr, C. E., Wasserman, R. H., Gray, J. R., Greve, D. N., Treadway, M. T., & McGarvey, M. (2005, November 28). Meditation experience is associated with increased cortical thickness. Retrieved from http://www.ncbi.nlm.nih.gov/pmc/articles/PMC1361002/

26 Hölzel, B. K., Carmody, J. C., Vangel,, M., Congleton, C., Yerramsetti, S. M., Gard, T., & Lazar, S. W. (2011, January 30). Mindfulness practice leads to increases in regional brain gray matter density. Retrieved from http://www.ncbi.nlm.nih.gov/pmc/articles/PMC3004979/?_escaped_fragment_=po=1.72414

27 Gard, T., Hölzel, B. K., & Sara W. Lazar, S. W. (2014, January 13). The potential effects of meditation on age-related cognitive decline: a systematic review - Gard - 2014 - Annals of the New York Academy of Sciences - Wiley Online Library. Retrieved from http://onlinelibrary.wiley.com/doi/10.1111/nyas.12348/abstract

28 Newberg, A. B., Serruya, M., Wintering, N., Moss, A. S., Reibel, D., & Monti, D. A. (2013, August 7). Meditation and neurodegenerative diseases - Newberg - 2013 - Annals of the New York Academy of Sciences - Wiley Online Library. Retrieved from http://onlinelibrary.wiley.com/doi/10.1111/nyas.12187/abstract

29 Seth, A. K., Suzuki, K., & Critchley, H. D. (2012, January 10). An Interoceptive Predictive Coding Model of Conscious Presence. Retrieved from http://www.ncbi.nlm.nih.gov/pmc/articles/PMC3254200/

30 Such as:

Mark Wheeler, M. (2012, March 14). Evidence builds that meditation strengthens the brain, UCLA researchers say | UCLA. Retrieved from http://newsroom.ucla.edu/releases/evidence-builds-that-meditation-230237, and Land, D. (2008, March 25). Study shows compassion meditation changes the brain. Retrieved from http://www.news.wisc.edu/14944

31 Singer, T., Seymour, B., Doherty, R. J., & Dolan, C. D. (2004). Empathy for Pain Involves the Affective but not Sesory Components of Pain. *Science*, *303*, 1157-1162. doi:10.1126/science.1093535

32 See the image here: http://www.joostrekveld.net/wp/wp-content/uploads/2007/03/bach-y-rita1.jpg

33 There is a great video about this: Bach-y-Rita, P. (2013, July). *Neuroplasticity on Vimeo* [Video file]. Retrieved from http://vimeo.com/59755393

34 Schmidt-Wilckea, T., Rosengarth, K., Luerdinga, R., Bogdahna, U., & Greenlee, M. W. (2010, July 1). Distinct patterns of functional and structural neuroplasticity associated with learning Morse code. Retrieved from http://www.sciencedirect.com/science/article/pii/S1053811910003290

35 Maguire, E. A., Frackowiak RS, R. S., & Frith, C. D. (1997, September 15). Recalling routes around london: activation of the right hippocampus in taxi drivers. - PubMed - NCBI. Retrieved from http://www.ncbi.nlm.nih.gov/pubmed/9278544

36 Maguire, E. (2000, March 14). BBC NEWS | Science/Nature | Taxi drivers' brains 'grow' on the job. Retrieved from http://news.bbc.co.uk/2/hi/677048.stm

37 Britta, B. K., Carmody, J., Vangel, M., Congleton, C., Yerramesetti, S. M., Gard, T., & Lazara, S. W. (2011, January 30). Mindfulness practice leads to increases in regional brain gray matter density. Retrieved from http://www.ncbi.nlm.nih.gov/pmc/articles/PMC3004979/

38 Pali is the scriptural tongue of early Buddhism, a close cognate to the language that the historical Buddha is thought to have spoken. It is probably some form of Middle Indo-Aryan, but nobody really knows. There is an enormous volume of early Buddhist writings in the Pali language, and for that reason it remains important.

39 An interesting example is a practice found in the Eastern Orthodox Christian tradition, known as *omphaloskepsis*, or contemplation of the navel. This is a kind of mindfulness practice, involving gazing at the belly and feeling the body sensations there. Roman Catholic Christians found this practice comical, and derided it as useless, which is where we get the phrase "navel gazing."

40 Wilson, T., Reinhard, D. A., Westgate, E. C., Gilbert, D. T., Ellerbeck, N., Hahn, C., & Brown, C. L. (2014, July 4). Just think: The challenges of the disengaged mind. Retrieved from www.sciencemag.org/content/345/6192

41 Killingsworth, M. A., & Gilbert, D. T. (2010). A Wandering Mind Is an Unhappy Mind. *Science*, *330*, 1-6. doi:10.1126/science.1192439

42 Creswell, J. D., Eisenberger, B. M., & Lieberman, N. I. (2007, July 18). Neural correlates of dispositional mindfulness during affect labeling. - PubMed - NCBI. Retrieved from http://www.ncbi.nlm.nih.gov/pubmed/17634566

43 https://youtu.be/8NPzLBSBzPI

44 Carney, D. R., Cuddy, A. J., & Yapp, A. J. (2010, January 20). Power Posing. Retrieved from http://pss.sagepub.com/content/21/10/1363.short

45 Libet, etc.

46 Besides the studies noted earlier, see: Zeidan, F., Johnson, S. K., Diamond, B. J., David, Z., & Goolkasian, P. (2010). Mindfulness meditation improves cognition: Evidence of brief mental training. *Consciousness and Cognition*, *1*(1), 1-9. doi:10.1016/j.concog.2010.03.014

47 A really good example of this: MacLean, K. A., Ferrer, E., Aichele, S. R., Bridwell, D. A., Zanesco, A. P., & Jacobs, T. L. (2010, June 21). Intensive meditation training improves perceptual discrimination and sustained attention. - PubMed - NCBI. Retrieved from http://www.ncbi.nlm.nih.gov/pubmed/20483826

48http://himalayanconnections.org/wp-content/uploads/pdf/Mrazek_2013_Mindfulness%20mprovesWMCandGRD_PschSci.pdf

49 These numbers are just pseudo-math, for the purpose of illustration, of course. However, the effects of mindfulness meditation on increased sensory clarity have been demonstrated. For example: Fell, A. (2013, March 27). Mindfulness from meditation associated with lower stress hormone :: UC Davis News & Information. Retrieved from http://www.news.ucdavis.edu/search/news_detail.lasso?id=10538studies/sites/brown.edu.academics.contempl ative-studies/files/uploads/Kerr_alpha_modulation_meditation_2011.pdf

50 Leeuwen, S. V., Singer, W., & Melloni, L. (2012, May 15). Meditation Increases the Depth of Information Processing and Improves the Allocation of Attention in Space. Retrieved from http://www.ncbi.nlm.nih.gov/pmc/articles/PMC3351800/

51 Fox, K. C., Zakarauskas, P., Dixon, M., Ellamil, M., Thompson, E., & Christoff, K. (2012, September 25). Meditation Experience Predicts Introspective Accuracy. Retrieved from http://www.ncbi.nlm.nih.gov/pmc/articles/PMC3458044/

52 In traditional Buddhist practice, as well as Shinzen's Basic Mindfulness School, this third element is called "equanimity." I've found that term doesn't resonate well with my students. The term "acceptance" is, in my opinion, more to the point.

53 Kerr, C. E., Josyula, K., & Littenberg, R. (2012, January 1). Developing an observing attitude: A qualitative analysis of meditation diaries in a MBSR clinical trial. Retrieved from http://www.ncbi.nlm.nih.gov/pmc/articles/PMC3032385/

54 Teper, R., & Inzlicht, M. (2011, October 20). Meditation, mindfulness, and executive control: the importance of emotional acceptance and brain-based performance monitoring. Retrieved from http://scan.oxfordjournals.org/content/8/1/85.full

55 Soon, C. S., Brass, M., Heinze, H. J., & Haynes, J. D. (2008, April 13). Access : Unconscious determinants of free decisions in the human brain : Nature Neuroscience. Retrieved from http://www.nature.com/neuro/journal/v11/n5/full/nn.2112.html

56 The scientist whose work Gladwell used as the basis for his idea disputes Gladwell's conclusions. Ericsson, K. A. (2014, July). Why expert performance is special and cannot be extrapolated from studies of performance in the general population: A response to criticisms. Retrieved from http://www.sciencedirect.com/science/article/pii/S0160289613001736

57 by Theodosius Dobzhansky

58 Using DNA for species delimitation, with an understanding of how genes mutate, for example, is fixing some areas of taxonomy which were based on morphology.

59 Zimmer, C. (2010, September 3). The Worm In Your Brain - The Loom : The Loom. Retrieved from http://blogs.discovermagazine.com/loom/2010/09/03/the-worm-in-your-brain/#.VOOv_FPF874

60 Brain structures devoted to learning, memory highly conserved in animal kingdom, suggesting common evolutionary origin. (2014, December 18). Retrieved from http://phys.org/news/2014-12-brain-devoted-memory-highly-animal.html

61 You can rest assured that I know that evolution didn't happen on purpose.

62 Price, T. J., & Dussor, G. (2011, April 11). Retrieved from www.sciencedirect.com/science/article/pii/S0960982214004114

63 Fernando, A. B., Murray, J. E., & Milton, A. L. (2013, December 6). The amygdala: securing pleasure and avoiding pain. - PubMed - NCBI. Retrieved from http://www.ncbi.nlm.nih.gov/pubmed/24367307

64 Due to fever.

65 Material on Roberto Salazar reprinted from the book *Ego*, by Peter Bauman and Michael W. Taft. Baumann, P & Taft, M. *Ego: The Fall of the Twin Towers and the Rise of an Enlightened Humanity*. San Francisco, CA: NE, 2011. Print.

66 Rhudy, J. L., & Meagher, M. W. (2000, January). Fear and anxiety: divergent effects on human pain thresholds. Retrieved from http://www.sciencedirect.com/science/article/pii/S0304395999001839

67 Zeidan, F., Martucci, K. T., Kraft, R. A., Gordon, N. S., McHaffie, J. G., & Coghill, R. C. (2011). Brain Mechanisms Supporting the Modulation of Pain by Mindfulness Meditation. *The Journal of Neuroscience*, *31*(14), 5540-5548.

68 Denver, R. J. (2009, April 1). Structural and functional evolution of vertebrate neuroendocrine stress systems. - PubMed - NCBI. Retrieved from http://www.ncbi.nlm.nih.gov/pubmed/19456324

69 Wilhelm, I., Wagner, U., & Born, J. (2011, December). MIT Press Journals - Journal of Cognitive Neuroscience - Abstract. Retrieved from http://www.mitpressjournals.org/doi/abs/10.1162/jocn_a_00093#.VPZKf1PF875

70 This is speculation on my part. Our nervous system, however, seems to be optimized for such a routine. Acute stress is much more tolerable than chronic stress.

71 There is some debate about how unique it really is: Suddendorf, T., & Corballis, M. C. (2007). Behavioral and Brain Sciences - Abstract - The evolution of foresight: What is mental time travel, and is it unique to humans? Retrieved from http://journals

72 Sapolsky, R. M. (2012, March 22). How to Relieve Stress | Greater Good. Retrieved from http://greatergood.berkeley.edu/article/item/how_to_relieve_stress

73 Consistency theory mainly predicts that people want to appear consistent so badly that they will lie about, deny, or dissemble (even to themselves) about the actuality of what they said previously.

74 http://www.rainlendar.net/cms/index.php

75 http://www.appigo.com/

76 Here are a few good mindfulness apps:

The Mindfulness App ($1.99)
Iphone - https://itunes.apple.com/us/app/the-mindfulness-app/id417071430
Android - https://play.google.com/store/apps/details?id=se.lichtenstein.mind.en

Get Some Headspace (Free)
Iphone - https://itunes.apple.com/us/app/headspace-on-the-go/id493145008?mtt=8
Android - https://play.google.com/store/apps/details?id=com.getsomeheadspace.android

Buddhist Meditation Trainer (Free reminder app)
Andoid - https://play.google.com/store/apps/details?id=com.bmt&hl=en

77 Mindfulness Group Resources
https://www.Meetup.com (Search Mindfulness, Meditation, and/or Mindfulness Meditation)

http://www.buddhistinsightnetwork.org/sanghas

78 Grant, J. A., Courtemanche, J., & Rainville, P. (2011). A non-elaborative mental stance and decoupling of executive and pain-related cortices predicts low pain sensitivity in Zen meditators. PAIN®, 152(1), 150-156.

79 Gard T, Holzel BK, Sack AT, Hempel H, Vaitl D, Ott U. Pain attenuation through mindfulness is associated with decreased cognitive control and increased sensory processing in the brain.

Specifically, What they show is that brain activation in secondary somatosensory cortex (SII) and posterior insula (associated with the sensory domain of pain processing) greater in mindfulness than a baseline condition correlates with decreasing pain unpleasantness in mindfulness practitioners, but increasing pain unpleasantness in controls.

80 Notably Han Solo: "It's all a lot of simple tricks and nonsense."

81)Damasio, A. R. (1999). The feeling of what happens: Body and emotion in the making of consciousness. New York: Harcourt Brace.

2)Davidson, R. J. (1994). Complexities in the search for emotion-specific physiology. In P. Ekman & R. J. Davidson (Eds.), The nature of emotion: Fundamental questions(pp. 237–242). New York: Oxford University Press.

3)Panksepp, J. (1998). Affective neuroscience: The foundations of human and animal emotions. New York: Oxford University Press.

82 Here's a free online version of the entire book. http://www.gutenberg.org/files/1227/1227-h/1227-h.htm

83 Yes, even though it's *still* heretical to suggest it, it seems pretty clear that animals have emotions—given that they have similar brain structures, similar neurochemistry, and similar behaviors under similar conditions, calling them "sham emotions" like the behaviorists did seems like splitting hairs.

84 Brickman, Philip; Coates, Dan; Janof-BUlman, Ronnie, Aug, 1978, Journal of Personality and Social psychology 36.8, 917-927

85 Damasio, "Descartes' Error" 1994

86 Panksepp, J., & Northoff, G. (2009, March 18). The trans-species core SELF: the emergence of active cultural and neuro-ecological agents through self-related processing within subcortical-cortic... - PubMed - NCBI. Retrieved from http://www.ncbi.nlm.nih.gov/pubmed/18485741

87 Davis, J. I., Senghas, A., Brandt, F., & Ochsner, K. N. (2013, July 10). The Effects of BOTOX® Injections on Emotional Experience. Retrieved from http://www.ncbi.nlm.nih.gov/pmc/articles/PMC2880828/

88 Neal, D. (2011, October 31). Embodied Emotion Perception: Amplifying and Dampening Facial Feedback Modulates Emotion Perception Accuracy. Retrieved from http://spp.sagepub.com/content/early/2011/04/21/1948550611406138.abstract

89 ibid

90 Britta, B. K., Carmody, J., Vangel, M., Congleton, C., Yerramesetti, S. M., Gard, T., & Lazara, S. W. (2011, January 30). Mindfulness practice leads to increases in regional brain gray matter density. Retrieved from http://www.ncbi.nlm.nih.gov/pmc/articles/PMC3004979/

91 As shown by alpha modulation in the primary somatosensory cortex by Cathy Kerr Kerr, C. E., Jones, S. R., Wan, Q., Pritchett, D. L., Wasserman, R. H., Wexler, A., . . . Moore, C. I. (2011). Effects of mindfulness meditation training on anticipatory alpha modulation in primary somatosensory cortex. FUEL AND ENERGY ABSTRACTS, 1-8. doi:10.1016/j.brainresbull.2011.03.026

92 Ozbay, F., Fitterling, H., Charney, D., & Southwick, S. (2008). Social support and resilience to stress across the life span: a neurobiologic framework. *Current psychiatry reports*, *10*(4), 304-310. Retrieved from http://link.springer.com/article/10.1007/s11920-008-0049-7

93 Strack, F., Martin, L. L., & Stepper, S. (1988). Inhibiting and facilitating conditions of the human smile: A nonobtrusive test of the facial feedback hypothesis. JOURNAL OF PERSONALITY AND SOCIAL PSYCHOLOGY, 54(5), 768-777. doi:10.1037//0022-3514.54.5.768

94 Many of the lines were cribbed from a book entitled, *The Conspiracy Against the Human Race,* which espouses the view that life is so awful it is better to never have been born. I certainly do not subscribe to this view.

95 Ray Bradbury: Writer, 1920-2012 | Harvard Square Library. (2000, November). Retrieved from http://www.harvardsquarelibrary.org/biographies/ray-bradbury/

96 from My Life and the Beautiful Game: The Autobiography of Pele, By Pele, Robert L. Fish, Shep Messing

97 http://archive.wired.com/wired/archive/4.09/czik_pr.html

98 Psygrammer |. (2011, February 10). The Flow – Programming in Ecstasy | Psygrammer. Retrieved from **http://psygrammer.com/2011/02/10/the-flow-programming-in-ecstasy/**

99Richard Chambers, Barbara Chuen Yee Lo, Nicholas B. Allen, R., Yee Lo, B. C., & Allen, N. (2007, February 23). The Impact of Intensive Mindfulness Training on Attentional Control, Cognitive Style, and Affect - Springer. Retrieved from http://link.springer.com/article/10.1007%2Fs10608-007-9119-0#page-1

Tang, Y., & Posner, M. I. (2015). Mindfulness in the context of the attention system. In K. W. Brown, J. D. Creswell, R. M. Ryan, K. W. Brown, J. D. Creswell, R. M. Ryan (Eds.) , *Handbook of mindfulness: Theory, research, and practice* (pp. 81-89). New York, NY, US: Guilford Press.

Valentine, E. R., & Sweet, P. L. (1999). Meditation and attention: A comparison of the effects of concentrative and mindfulness meditation on sustained attention. *Mental Health, Religion & Culture, 2*(1), 59-70. Retrieved from http://www.tandfonline.com/doi/abs/10.1080/13674679908406332#.Va6WiUVedcw

Jha, A. P., Krompinger, J., & Baime, M. J. (2007). Mindfulness training modifies subsystems of attention. *Cognitive, Affective, & Behavioral Neuroscience, 7*(2), 109-119. Retrieved from http://link.springer.com/article/10.3758/CABN.7.2.109

100 http://www.pnas.org/content/104/27/11483.full

101 http://www.pnas.org/content/104/43/17152.short

102 http://www.cell.com/trends/cognitive-sciences/abstract/S1364-6613(03)00028-7?_returnURL=http%3A%2F%2Flinkinghub.elsevier.com%2Fretrieve%2Fpii%2FS1364661303000287%3Fshowall%3Dtrue

103 http://www.slate.com/articles/health_and_science/science/2009/08/seeking.html

104 The fact that we're not sure if something awesome will show up this time makes it even more addictive (see the fascinating video below).

DOPAMINE JACKPOT! SAPOLSKY ON THE SCIENCE OF PLEASURE [Video file]. (2011, May 2). Retrieved from http://www.youtube.com/watch?feature=player_embedded&v=axrywDP9Ii0

105 https://youtu.be/1KaOrSuWZeM

106 A paraphrase of the *Communist Manifesto* by Karl Marx and Friedrich Engels.

107 Yes, I'm making a speciesist statement. I could be wrong about the consciousness level of fungi and bacteria, but you get the point.

108 Thank you to Maria Konnikova whose article about *Dune* and Positive Thinking reminded me of this epic scene in the book. Konnikova, M. (2012, February 9). WHAT FRANK HERBERT'S DUNE CAN TEACH US ABOUT THE POWER OF POSITIVE THINKING. Retrieved from http://io9.com/5883825/what-frank-herberts-dune-can-teach-us-about-the-power-of-positive-thinking

109 Law, W., & Man, R. (2011). An Analogue Study of Loving-Kindness Meditation as a Buffer against Social Stress - The University of Arizona Campus Repository. Retrieved from http://arizona.openrepository.com/arizona/handle/10150/145398

110 Pace, Ph.D, T. W., Negi, Ph.D., L. T., Adame, Ph.D., D. D., Cole, Ph.D., S. P., Sivilli, T. I., Brown, M.P.H., T. D., & Issa, M. J. (2009, January). Effect of Compassion Meditation on Neuroendocrine, Innate Immune and Behavioral Responses to Psychosocial Stress. Retrieved from http://www.ncbi.nlm.nih.gov/pmc/articles/PMC2695992/

111 Hoge EA1, Chen MM, Orr E, Metcalf CA, Fischer LE, Pollack MH, De Vivo I, Simon NM., E. A., Chen, M. M., Orr, E., Metcalf, C. A., Fischer, L. E., Pollack, M. H., & Vivo, D. I. (2013, August). Loving-Kindness Meditation practice associated with longer telomeres in women. - PubMed - NCBI. Retrieved from http://www.ncbi.nlm.nih.gov/pubmed/23602876

112 Kearney, D. J., Malte, C. A., McManus, C., Martinez, M. E., & Felleman, B. (2013, August 26). Loving-kindness meditation for posttraumatic stress disorder: a pilot study. - PubMed - NCBI. Retrieved from http://www.ncbi.nlm.nih.gov/pubmed/23893519

113 Fredrickson, B. L., Cohn, M. A., Coffey, K. A., Pek, J., & Finkel, S. M. (2011, August 15). Open Hearts Build Lives: Positive Emotions, Induced Through Loving-Kindness Meditation, Build Consequential Personal Resources. Retrieved from http://www.ncbi.nlm.nih.gov/pmc/articles/PMC3156028/

114 Kok, B. E., Coffey, K. A., Cohn, M. A., Catalino, L. I., Vacharkulksemsuk, T., Algoe, S. B., & Brantley, M. (2013, July 1). How positive emotions build physical health: perceived positive social connections account for the upward spiral between positive emotions and vaga... - PubMed - NCBI. Retrieved from http://www.ncbi.nlm.nih.gov/pubmed/23649562

115 Tonelli, M. E., & Wachholtz, A. B. (2014, March 15). Meditation-based treatment yielding immediate relief for meditation-naïve migraineurs. - PubMed - NCBI. Retrieved from http://www.ncbi.nlm.nih.gov/pubmed/24602422

116 Carson, J. W., Keefe, F. J., Lynch, T. R., Carson, K. M., Goli, V., Fras, A. M., & Thorp, S. R. (2005, September 23). Loving-kindness meditation for chronic low back pain: results from a pilot trial. - PubMed - NCBI. Retrieved from http://www.ncbi.nlm.nih.gov/pubmed/16049118

117 Compassion Meditation May Improve Physical And Emotional Responses To Psychological Stress -- ScienceDaily. (2008, October 7). Retrieved from http://www.sciencedaily.com/releases/2008/10/081007172902.htm

118 Veenhoven, R. (2008). Healthy happiness: effects of happiness on physical health and the consequences for preventive health care. JOURNAL OF HAPPINESS STUDIES, 9, 449–469. doi:10.1007/s10902-006-9042-1

119 Kubzansky, L. D., Sparrow, D., Vokonas, P., & Kawachi, I. (2001, November). Is the glass half empty or half full? A prospective study of optimism and coronary heart disease in the normative aging study. - PubMed - NCBI. Retrieved from http://www.ncbi.nlm.nih.gov/pubmed/11719629/

120 Tugade, M. M., Fredrickson, B. L., & Barrett, L. F. (2004, December). Psychological Resilience and Positive Emotional Granularity: Examining the Benefits of Positive Emotions on Coping and Health. Retrieved from http://www.ncbi.nlm.nih.gov/pmc/articles/PMC1201429/#R73

121 Gawande, A. (2009, March 30). Is Long-Term Solitary Confinement Torture? - The New Yorker. Retrieved from http://www.newyorker.com/magazine/2009/03/30/hellhole

122 Empathy and compassion appear to be two very different systems in the brain (see the research of Tania Singer). Furthermore, altruism refers to behavior, not feelings. However, for the sake of easier reading, I'm going to use all three terms somewhat interchangeably here.

123 Hublin, J. J. (2013, December 24). The prehistory of compassion. Retrieved from http://www.pnas.org/content/106/16/6429.full

124 Beckes, L., Coan, J. A., & Hasselmo, K. (2011, September 16). Familiarity promotes the blurring of self and other in the neural representation of threat. Retrieved from http://scan.oxfordjournals.org/content/8/6/670.abstract?sid=c4150ef8-e979-4413-a3e0-2b067a6e65af

125 Jaremka, L. M., Fagundes, C. P., Peng, J., Bennett, J. M., Glaser, R., Malarkey, W. B., & Kiecolt-Glaser, J. K. (2013). Loneliness promotes inflammation during acute stress. *Psychological science*, *24*(7), 1089-1097. Retrieved from http://pss.sagepub.com/content/24/7/1089.abstract

126 Moskowitz, C. (2008, September 16). Social Isolation Makes People Cold, Literally. Retrieved from http://www.livescience.com/5090-social-isolation-people-cold-literally.html

127 Holt-Lunstad, J., Smith, T. B., Barker, M., Harris, T., & Stephenson, D. (2015, March 1). Loneliness and Social Isolation as Risk Factors for Mortality. Retrieved from http://pps.sagepub.com/content/10/2/227.abstract

128 Theodoridou, A., Rowe, A. C., Penton-Voak, I. S., & Rogers, P. J. (2009, March 19). Oxytocin and social perception: Oxytocin increases perceived facial trustworthiness and attractiveness. Retrieved from http://www.sciencedirect.com/science/article/pii/S0018506X09000853

129 Hurlemann R, Patin A, Onur OA, Cohen MX, Baumgartner T, Metzler S, Dziobek I, Gallinat J, Wagner M, Maier W, Kendrick KM (April 2010). "Oxytocin enhances amygdala-dependent, socially reinforced learning and emotional empathy in humans". *J. Neurosci.* **30** (14): 4999–5007.

130 Zak, P. J., Stanton, A. A., & Ahmadi, S. (2007, November 7). PLOS ONE: Oxytocin Increases Generosity in Humans. Retrieved from http://journals.plos.org/plosone/article?id=10.1371/journal.pone.0001128

131 Crawley, J. N., Chen, T., Puri, A., Washburn, R., Sullivan, T. L., Hill, J. M., & Young, N. B. (2007, February 2). Social approach behaviors in oxytocin knockout mice: Comparison of two independent lines tested in different laboratory environments. Retrieved from www.neuropeptidesjournal.com/article/S0143-4179(07)00017-0/abstract

132 Guastella, A. J., Mitchell, P. B., & Mathews, F. (2013, February 13). Oxytocin Enhances the Encoding of Positive Social Memories in Humans. Retrieved from www.biologicalpsychiatryjournal.com/article/S0006-3223(08)00188-1/abstract

133 Rimmele, U., Hediger, K., Heinrichs, M., & Klaver, P. (2009, January 7). Oxytocin Makes a Face in Memory Familiar. Retrieved from http://www.jneurosci.org/content/29/1/38

134 Carmichael, M. S., Humbert, R. D., Palmisano, G., Greenleaf, W., & Davidson, J. M. (1987, January). Plasma oxytocin increases in the human sexual response. - PubMed - NCBI. Retrieved from http://www.ncbi.nlm.nih.gov/pubmed/3782434/

135 Marazziti, D., Dell'Osso, B., Baroni, S., Mungai, F., Catena, M., Rucci, P., . . . Albanese, F. (2006, October 11). A relationship between oxytocin and anxiety of romantic attachment. Retrieved from http://www.ncbi.nlm.nih.gov/pmc/articles/PMC1621060/

136 Scheele, D., Striepens, N., Güntürkün, O., Deutschländer, S., Maier, W., Kendrick, K. M., & Hurlemann, R. (2012, November 14). Oxytocin Modulates Social Distance between Males and Females. Retrieved from http://www.jneurosci.org/content/32/46/16074

137 Hartwig, Walenty (1989). *Endokrynologia praktyczna*. Warsaw: Państwowy Zakład Wydawnictw Lekarskich. ISBN 83-200-1415-8

138 Viviani, D., Charlet, A., Burg, E. V., Robinet, C., Hurni, N., Abatis, M., . . . Magara, F. (2011, July 1). Oxytocin Selectively Gates Fear Responses Through Distinct Outputs from the Central Amygdala. Retrieved from http://www.sciencemag.org/content/333/6038/104

139 Heinrich, M., Baumgartner, T., Kirschbaum, C., & Ehlert, U. (2003, April 17). Social support and oxytocin interact to suppress cortisol and subjective responses to psychosocial stress - Biological Psychiatry. Retrieved from http://www.biologicalpsychiatryjournal.com/article/S0006-3223(03)00465-7/abstract

140 Gouin, J., Carter, C. S., Pournajafi-Nazarloo, H., Glaser, R., Malarkey, W. B., Loving, T. J., & Stowell, J. (2009, October 17). Marital behavior, oxytocin, vasopressin, and wound healing - Psychoneuroendocrinology. Retrieved from http://www.psyneuen-journal.com/article/S0306-4530(10)00025-9/abstract

141 Barraza, J., & Zak, P. (2009, June 24). Empathy toward Strangers Triggers Oxytocin Release and Subsequent Generosity - Barraza - 2009 - Annals of the New York Academy of Sciences - Wiley Online Library. Retrieved from http://onlinelibrary.wiley.com/doi/10.1111/j.1749-6632.2009.04504.x/abstract

142 Hanson, Ph.D., R. (2010, July 20). Psychology.com Articles » Blog Archive » The Evolution of Love. Retrieved from http://www.psychology.com/articles/?p=198

143 Papers — Folding@home. (2014, January 27). Retrieved from http://folding.stanford.edu/home/papers

144 http://www.wjh.harvard.edu/~dtg/KILLINGSWORTH%20&%20GILBERT%20(2010).pdf

145 Brewer, J. A., Worhunsky, P. D., Gray, J. R., Tang, Y., Weber, J., & Kobera, H. (2011, December 13). Meditation experience is associated with differences in default mode network activity and connectivity. Retrieved from http://www.ncbi.nlm.nih.gov/pmc/articles/PMC3250176/

146 Cacioppo, J., & Frebert, L. A. (2015, January 1). *Discovering Psychology: The Science of Mind - John Cacioppo, Laura Freberg - Google Books*. Retrieved from https://books.google.com/books?id=tsrvBQAAQBAJ&lpg=PT236&ots=6_1ThCvYad&dq=dmn%20mistakes%2030%20seconds%20attention&pg=PT236#v=onepage&q=dmn%20mistakes%2030%20seconds%20attention&f=false

147 Watanabe, T., Kan, S., Koike, T., Misaki, M., Konishi, S., Miyauchi, S., & ... Masuda, N. (2014). Network-dependent modulation of brain activity during sleep. *Neuroimage*, 98 1-10. doi:10.1016/j.neuroimage.2014.04.0

Shepovalnikov, A. N., Tsitseroshin, M. N., Galperina, E. I., Rozhkov, V. P., Kruchinina, O. V., Zaitseva, L. G., & Panasevich, E. A. (2012). Characteristics of integrative brain activity during various stages of sleep and in transitional states. *Human Physiology*, 38(3), 227-237. doi:10.1134/S0362119712030127

148 Buckner RL, Andrews-Hanna JR, Schacter DL (2008) in *The Year in Cognitive Neuroscience 2008*, The brain's default network: Anatomy, function, and relevance to disease, eds Kingstone A, Miller MB(Blackwell Publishing, Malden, MA), pp 1–38

149 Kühn, S., Ritter, S. M., Muller, B. C., Van Baaren, R. B., Brass, M., & Dijksterhuis3, A. P. (2013, December 12). The Importance of the Default Mode Network in Creativity—A Structural MRI Study - Kühn - 2013 - The Journal of Creative Behavior - Wiley Online Library. Retrieved from http://onlinelibrary.wiley.com/doi/10.1002/jocb.45/abstract

150 Kaufman, S. B. (2013, December 23). The Real Link Between Creativity and Mental Illness | Scott Barry Kaufman. Retrieved from http://www.huffingtonpost.com/scott-barry-kaufman/the-real-link-between-cre_b_4149064.html

Takeuchi, H., Taki, Y., Hashizume, H., Sassa, Y., Nagase, T., Nouchi, R., & Kawashima, R. (2011). Failing to deactivate: the association between brain activity during a working memory task and creativity. *Neuroimage*, *55*(2), 681-687. Retrieved from http://www.sciencedirect.com/science/article/pii/S1053811910015302

Kühn, S., Ritter, S. M., Müller, B. C., Baaren, R. B., Brass, M., & Dijksterhuis, A. (2014). The importance of the default mode network in creativity—a structural MRI study. *The Journal of Creative Behavior*, *48*(2), 152-163. Retrieved from http://onlinelibrary.wiley.com/doi/10.1002/jocb.45/abstract

Fink, A., Weber, B., Koschutnig, K., Benedek, M., Reishofer, G., Ebner, F., ... & Weiss, E. M. (2014). Creativity and schizotypy from the neuroscience perspective. *Cognitive, Affective, & Behavioral Neuroscience*, *14*(1), 378-387. Retrieved from http://scottbarrykaufman.com/wp-content/uploads/2013/10/Fink-et-al.-2013.pdf

151 Ostafin, B. D., & Kassman, K. T. (2012). Stepping out of history: Mindfulness improves insight problem solving. *Consciousness And Cognition: An International Journal*, *21*(2), 1031-1036. doi:10.1016/j.concog.2012.02.014

Capurso, V., Fabbro, F., & Crescentini, C. (2014). Mindful creativity: The influence of mindfulness meditation on creative thinking. *Frontiers In Psychology*, *4*doi:10.3389/fpsyg.2013.01020

152 Hélie, S., & Sun, R. (2010, December 2). New psychology theory enables computers to mimic human creativity. Retrieved from http://www.sciencedaily.com/releases/2010/12/101201124345.htm

153 Brewer, Ph.D., J. (2014, January 14). Is Mindfulness Harmful? Retrieved from http://www.huffingtonpost.com/dr-judson-brewer/mindfulness-practice_b_4602714.html

154 Garrison, K. A., Santoyo, J. F., Davis, J. H., Thornhill, T. A., Kerr, C. E., & Brewer, J. A. (2013, August 6). Effortless awareness: using real time neurofeedback to investigate correlates of posterior cingulate cortex activity in meditators' self-report. Retrieved from http://www.ncbi.nlm.nih.gov/pmc/articles/PMC3734786/

25651158R00136

Made in the USA
San Bernardino, CA
06 November 2015